FINANCIAL ORIGAMI

Since 1996, Bloomberg Press has published books for financial professionals, as well as books of general interest in investing, economics, current affairs, and policy affecting investors and business people. Titles are written by well-known practitioners, BLOOMBERG NEWS® reporters and columnists, and other leading authorities and journalists. Bloomberg Press books have been translated into more than 20 languages.

For a list of available titles, please visit our Web site at www.wiley.com/go/bloombergpress.

FINANCIAL ORIGAMI

How the Wall Street Model Broke

Brendan Moynihan

BLOOMBERG PRESS
An Imprint of
WILEY

Published by John Wiley & Sons, Inc., Hoboken, New Jersey.

Published simultaneously in Canada.

For general information on our other products and services or for technical support, please contact our Customer Care Department within the United States at (800) 762-2974, outside the United States at (317) 572-3993 or fax (317) 572-4002.

Wiley also publishes its books in a variety of electronic formats. Some content that appears in print may not be available in electronic books. For more information about Wiley products, visit our web site at www.wiley.com.

Library of Congress Cataloging-in-Publication Data
Moynihan, Brendan, author.
    Financial Origami : How the Wall Street Model Broke / Brendan Moynihan.
      p.   cm
    Includes index.
    ISBN 978-1-118-00181-3; ISBN 978-1-118-03030-1 (ebk); ISBN 978-1-118-03031-8 (ebk); ISBN 978-1-118-03032-5 (ebk)
      1. Financial engineering.   2. Financial risk.   3. Securities industry—United States.
    4. Global Financial Crisis, 2008–2009.   I. Title.
    HG176.7.M69 2011
    332.601—dc22
                                                                                    2010049551

Printed in the United States of America

10   9   8   7   6   5   4   3   2   1

To Kristiana, John, and Matthew

Contents

Contents

Author's Note

I t's been said that lower-class people talk about people; the middle class, things; and the upper class, ideas.

This book presents a few, simple ideas that explain the main events that shaped financial markets, firms, and products over the past 40 years and broke Wall Street over the past three. It examines the evolution of Wall Street, shows the logical sequence of events that brought us to this point, and presents some ideas for how to fix it.

Anyone looking for another book based on hours of interviews with anonymous people offering titillating tidbits about Washington and Wall Street will be sorely disappointed in the pages that follow. A similar letdown awaits anyone looking for another rehash of personalities, idiosyncrasies, expensive houses and cars, helicopters, and vacations. No "furrowed brow," "thought to himself," or "adrenaline coursing through her slender body" in this book.

Introduction

The simplicity of Wall Street has often been masked by the supposed complexity of the products it "engineers" and peddles to investors. "Engineer" is a big word, conjuring slide rule and pocket protectors for those of us old enough to remember them, and programmable calculators with built-in equations for those too young. What Wall Street calls financial engineering, I call Financial Origami, the art of paper-folding that uses a few, basic folds to shape pieces of paper into decorative models. Wall Street takes a few, basic pieces of paper stocks, bonds, and insurance contracts and folds their attributes together to make "new products," sometimes to skirt regulations, sometimes to meet investor needs, and always to boost profit. All of Wall Street's "innovations" are a function of how the attributes of these pieces of paper have been folded into something considered "new." Although the products look and sound complex, there is nothing new under Wall Street's sun. Grasping the origami involved in folding the same old pieces of paper will make understanding Wall Street and what happened in 2007–2009 easier than you think, and it will offer some insights on how to fix some of its problems.

Wall Street firms performed Financial Origami on more than just the products it has offered over the years. For decades through the 1960s, the firms had for the most part carried out distinct functions within the securities industry. Some specialized in advising and underwriting, others in sales, and still others in trading. Gradually, though, at punctuated points in time when the overall regulatory environment was changing, they began to refold the separate functions of the securities industry into single firms. But that's not all. They also refolded their business charters from private to public companies. And they would eventually unfold the mortgage origination process as well. All of these actions served to create *conflicts of interest* that reached epic proportions in the dot-com mania ending in 2000, and that reached Biblical proportions in 2007–2009. As we'll see, self-interest and conflicts of interest lie at the center of the financial crisis and hold the key for avoiding similar episodes in the future.

Former Federal Reserve Chairman Alan Greenspan started to address the topic in testimony before the House Committee on Oversight and Government Reform on October 23, 2008, and made what on the surface appeared to be a shocking admission:

> I made a mistake in presuming that the self-interest of organizations, specifically banks and others, were such that they were best capable of protecting their own shareholders and their equity in the firms. And it's been my experience, having worked both as a regulator for 18 years and similar quantities in the private sector, especially 10 years at a major international bank, that the loan officers of those institutions knew far more about the risks involved in the people to whom they lent money than I saw even our best regulators at the Fed capable of doing.

Lawmakers, pundits, and bloggers interpreted Greenspan as repudiating his free-market ideology. A *New York Times* headline screamed "Greenspan's Mea Culpa." The man most credited for the longest U.S.

economic expansion in history was now the most blamed for the sub-prime crisis. And it's nonsense. Not only did they misunderstand what he said, but they also missed a huge opportunity to address the role that self-interest and conflicts of interest played in the crisis.

During his 18 years as chairman of the Federal Reserve Board, ending in 2006, Alan Greenspan developed a reputation for delivering congressional testimony in so-called "Fedspeak," an opaque style of talking that seemed to baffle more than enlighten. He's been quoted as saying, "I know that you think you know what I said. But I'm not sure whether you understood that what you heard is what I meant." The October 2008 remarks are worth a closer examination. Organizations don't have self-interest; people do. An old axiom of economics is that people respond to incentives, and everything else is commentary. The individuals, salespeople, traders, loan officers, and CEOs were acting in their respective *self-interest,* prodded by the incentives in place at the time.

The month before Greenspan's testimony on the subprime crisis of 2007–2008, Lehman Brothers Holdings Inc. filed the largest bankruptcy in U.S. history, six times the size of the previous record-holder, Worldcom Inc., and ten times bigger than then second biggest, Enron Corp. Lehman's bankruptcy ended an era on Wall Street, one that stretched back more than the two or five or ten or even twenty years most have occupied themselves with when examining the financial crisis of 2007–2009. Identifying the right time frame is critical to understanding what happened on Wall Street and how we arrived at the financial crisis. Arbitrary designations will not do. Wall Street has odd notions about time. Measuring "year-to-date returns" is an arbitrary convention, and so is lumping together decades as though 10 years defined a unit with specific attributes: the eighties, nineties, or oughties, for example. Equally flawed are such starting points as contained in: "Stocks have returned an average of 10 percent a year since 1926." I've never met anyone who was investing in 1926 who is still alive today. Just because we have data on the

Standard & Poor's 500 Index going back that far doesn't mean that's a relevant starting point for comparisons.

At a minimum, it makes much more sense to define cyclical periods by economic recessions and expansions. For example: *How have stocks performed in expansions? What is the average performance during bull markets?* It makes even more sense to define secular periods using changes in monetary regimes because that is the largest factor influencing all the other decisions people make in markets, business, and the economy. It's logical to make broad statements about the post–World War II period because of the seminal financial regime changes that took place in 1946, right after the end of the war. The Employment Act of 1946 was a definitive attempt by the U.S. federal government to develop macroeconomic policy. The Bretton Woods Agreement bylaws establishing the international monetary system were adopted the same year, in the first global attempt at monetary cooperation on a permanent institutional basis.

At a maximum, perhaps, it makes sense to define secular periods in terms of the mobility of capital; that is, how freely does and can money circulate in the world economy. The most recent period of mobile global capital resembles the period starting in 1850 and ending in 1914,[1] the start

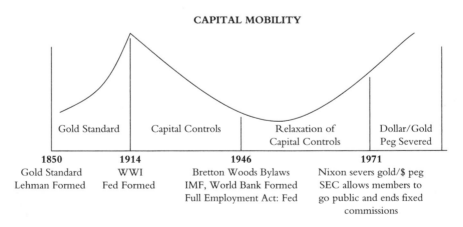

Figure I.1 Macroeconomic Stages of Capital Mobility and Capital Controls

of World War I and the first meeting of the Federal Reserve. In between the wars, the international capital movements collapsed as capital controls were imposed. From 1946 through 1971, capital controls were gradually relaxed, accompanied by a gradual recovery and capital flows. Figure I.1 shows the macro inflection points of capital mobility since 1850.

In 1850 several European governments adopted a silver currency system, leaving Britain as the only major currency in the world on the gold standard, just as the California Gold Rush dumped increased supply onto the market. Lehman Brothers formed in the same year, as a cotton merchant in Montgomery, Alabama. Its collapse 158 years later would trigger the biggest financial and economic crisis in the United States since at least the *original* Great Depression, the one in 1873. It would not be the last time Lehman or gold helped define an era.

SWAN

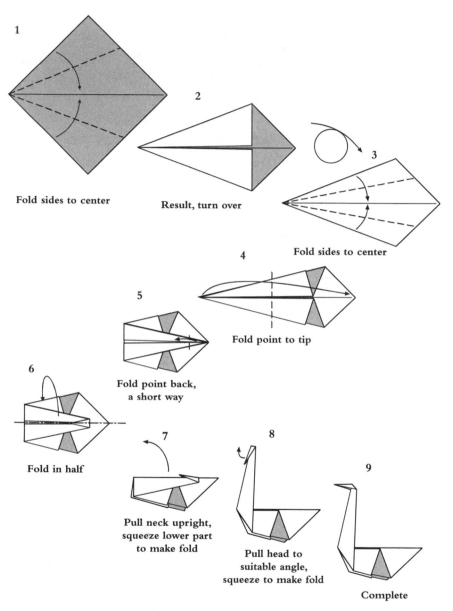

1 Fold sides to center

2 Result, turn over

3 Fold sides to center

4 Fold point to tip

5 Fold point back, a short way

6 Fold in half

7 Pull neck upright, squeeze lower part to make fold

8 Pull head to suitable angle, squeeze to make fold

9 Complete

Traditional Model © Diagrams D. Petty

FINANCIAL ORIGAMI

Chapter 1

Fold Sides to Center

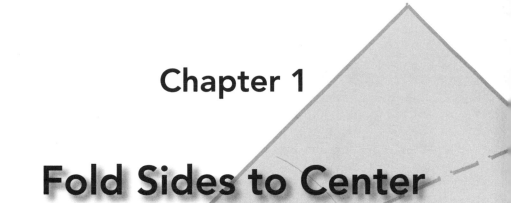

On September 16, 2008, investors in the Reserve Primary Fund, the world's first and oldest money market mutual fund, inundated the company with orders to redeem their shares and withdraw their cash. The Reserve was an alternative to a federally insured savings account or certificate of deposit at a bank. Over two days, shareholders pulled out more than 60 percent of the fund's $64.8 billion in assets. Many investors were unable to get to their money. And as of this writing, June 2010, many still are not.

The fund's shares had "broken the buck." That is, their net asset value had fallen below the $1 per share floor all such funds promise to maintain by investing in high-quality, short-term, interest-bearing securities. As long as the value of those securities does not fall below their promised payback amount—an unlikely event given the high credit rating and proximity to maturity—the money fund's shares are worth at least $1. The Reserve Fund, however, had invested in $785 million of debt from Lehman Brothers Holding Co., which filed for bankruptcy the day before.

It was the first time in history that a money fund designed for individuals had broken that threshold.[1] It was a so-called *Black Swan* event, a metaphor that Aristotle used more than 2,000 years ago to describe the "improbable," and popularized in 2007 in a best-selling book by the same title, by Nassim Nicholas Taleb.[2] Within a week, four of the five largest independent investment banks ceased to exist: Lehman Brothers filed for bankruptcy, Merrill Lynch & Co. sold to Bank of America, and Morgan Stanley & Co., and Goldman & Sachs Inc. became commercial bank holding companies. The fifth, Bear Stearns Cos., was sold to JPMorgan Chase six months earlier.

Baffled investors wondered, how could this happen? How could an investment bank file for bankruptcy, especially since the federal government six months earlier had arranged for the ailing investment bank Bear Stearns & Co. to be purchased by a commercial bank, JPMorgan Chase? How could the largest money fund in the world break the buck? How could the Wall Street business model break? If Wall Street is *broken,* can't we just go back to a time when it was *fixed*?

Flash back to the days just before the Reserve Primary Fund opened to the public for business on October 8, 1971, when plenty was fixed. The United States had a fixed exchange rate for the dollar, fixed interest-rate ceilings banks could pay on deposits, fixed-rate mortgages, fixed oil prices, and fixed commissions when buying and selling stocks on the New York Stock Exchange. The government had a fixed minimum investment in U.S. Treasury bills: $10,000. And that was real money, about $53,000 in 2010 dollars, when President Richard Nixon severed the link between the U.S. dollar and gold just two months before the Reserve Fund opened. Since the end of World War II, foreign central banks could exchange gold for dollars, and vice versa, at a fixed $35 per ounce. Nixon's move marked the first time in more than 2,000 years that a major world currency was not backed by a precious metal. There was even a fixed amount of gold U.S. citizens were allowed to hold of gold coin or bullion: zero. In 1933 Franklin Delano Roosevelt, in one of his first acts as president, issued executive order

6102, which made it illegal for U.S. citizens to own gold except for small amounts in jewelry. Under the Trading with the Enemy Act, violating the order was punishable by a fine of $10,000 (about $170,000 in 2010 dollars), up to 10 years in prison, or both. There was even a monetary reward offered for turning in people who failed to comply.

In this "fixed" environment, people had few alternatives for putting their savings to work. Generally, unspent money was deposited into a commercial bank such as Citibank, a savings and loan such as Glendale Federal S&L, or a securities firm such as Merrill Lynch. Tracing a deposit through these types of institutions helps reveal the flaws and conflicts of interest that developed over the past several decades, eventually breaking the Wall Street business model.

Commercial Banks

In 1971 median household income in the United States was about $10,000, which gave the typical family about $400 in savings at the end of the year.[3] Depositing the $400 into a savings account earned a maximum 5 and 3/4 percent, a fixed ceiling set by the Federal Reserve Board, the central bank of the United States. The government prohibited banks from paying interest on checking accounts. A certificate of deposit paid a maximum of 8 percent, fixed by the Federal Reserve.

Thousands of people would deposit money into a bank, which pooled the funds and lent them out to businesses or consumers. This effectively made the bank a clearinghouse, bringing savers and borrowers together and shifting the risk of holding cash to others who did not have enough for their purposes.

As required by law, before lending any of the deposits, the bank set aside 10 percent into a special account just in case the depositors wanted to make a withdrawal or write a check. If the bank had lent out all the funds, depositors would not have access to even a portion of their money. The set-aside was effectively *dead capital,* leaving the bank with only

90 percent of the deposit on which to earn enough to pay depositors and make a profit for itself. The notion of dead capital will arise in several other contexts in coming chapters; minimizing it, obviously, boosts profits for a bank and became an obsession in recent years.

If no one wanted to borrow or if the bank didn't want to lend to less-than-credit-worthy applicants, it alternatively could invest in U.S Treasury securities. It was able to pool the deposits to meet the Treasury's $10,000 minimum investment requirement. The bank would buy, say, $1,000,000 of two-year U.S. Treasury notes paying 6 percent per year. Each year, the bank would earn $60,000 in interest. If the bank's deposit rate was 3 percent, it would be paying its customers $30,000 a year. Carrying that position for the full two years would generate $30,000 in profit each year for the bank risk-free.

Banks lent to consumers and businesses, but they were only allowed to do so within state lines. Federal law, via the McFadden Act, prohibited interstate banking. Commercial bank deposits were federally insured up to $40,000. The Federal Reserve, through so-called Regulation Q (part of the 1933 Securities Act, also known as the Glass-Steagall Act), placed interest rate ceilings on saving accounts and CDs and prohibited paying interest on checking accounts.

The payments of interest and principal in bank accounts are federally insured by the Federal Depository Insurance Corporation (FDIC). All federally chartered commercial banks are required by law to pay insurance premiums into the fund, so all deposits up to a maximum ceiling are guaranteed. Federally insured deposits were a great idea, but they might provide incentives for banks to make reckless, irresponsible, or questionable loans. This raised the specter of so-called *moral hazard* whereby people behave more recklessly because they are not exposed to the full risk of their actions. Knowing that their deposit base was insured, bank officers might have incentives to make riskier loans than they would if they did not have the insurance.

So the government required banks to have some of the shareholders' money at risk to absorb any initial wave of losses on loans it might make.

It may not have removed moral hazard altogether, but at least the bank had some proverbial "skin in the game." This is akin to a potential homeowner having to have at least some money as a down payment as an equity interest in the property. So banks, and savings and loans for that matter, were required to set aside money for potential losses on the loans they made.

Familiarity with a bank savings account is all that's needed to understand how Wall Street prices its securities and derivatives. All a depositor needs to know is how to answer the following question: How much does a bank deposit of $100 grow to in one year at 5 percent interest? The simple math answer is $100 \times (1.05) = 105. Even if the depositor doesn't know, the bank teller can provide the answer. In fact, anyone capable of the simple arithmetic will calculate the *same* figure. The same is true for pricing the securities and derivatives in question: How much do I deposit into a bank account today at 5 percent interest in order to have $100 in the account in one year? Instead of *multiplying* to calculate future value, *divide* to get present value: $100/(1.05) = 95.24. That present value calculation on future streams of cash is how all financial instruments are priced. There is transparency in the savings account and a government guarantee of payment of interest and repayment of the principal. If the borrower of the money fails to make the promised interest payments and/ or failed to repay the loan, the depositor need not worry. Getting one's money back is certain.

Financial markets in 1971 were restrictive. Mortgages had fixed rates; no variable-rate products were offered. It took about a month for a banker to process a mortgage application. Once the loan was approved, the homeowner had to file updated annual financial statements to the bank. Additionally, the bank often conducted so-called drive-bys to view the upkeep of the property. A banker would literally drive past the property to see that it was in good repair, the lawn was mowed, and so on. The bank hadn't so much lent the money to buy the house as it had lent the house itself. If the homeowner failed to make monthly mortgage payments, the bank simply repossessed the house. Refinancing was rarely an option, as mortgages often had prepayment penalties. When buying a home, a buyer *could* get the lower rate of the current owner by "assuming the mortgage," making a down payment equal to the seller's equity in the house. First-time homebuyers were unlikely to match the equity of a seller who had lived in the house for 15 or 20 years, for example.

If depositors wanted to withdraw their money before those who had borrowed it from the bank paid it back, the bank would have to either call in some loans or else find some new depositors with enough money to repay the withdrawing depositors. If interest rates had risen in the meantime, the bank would have to offer higher, competitive rates to attract new depositors. The biggest risk was that market rates had risen above the ones the bank was receiving on its loans, so that the bank had to pay more for deposits than it was earning on loans or Treasury securities.

Thus banks brought together lenders and borrowers, shouldering the risk of short-term borrowing and longer-term lending. That maturity mismatch risk is a perennial problem for the financial industry. Nineteenth-century journalist and essayist Walter Bagehot addressed the phenomenon when he famously wrote, "The only securities which a banker using money that he may be asked at short notice to repay, ought to touch are those which are easily saleable and easily intelligible."[4]

Institutional investors such as insurance companies and pension funds could bypass the banks and lend directly to companies. These short-term loans, called commercial paper, are generally used for funding business operating expenses, such as to meet payrolls. They have a maximum of 270 days to maturity, which was a way of avoiding having to register the securities with the Securities and Exchange Commission. The rationale for allowing institutional investors to lend via commercial paper was that sophisticated investors didn't need as much government oversight or protection.

Savings and Loans

Deposits in a savings and loan were similar to the bank deposits, with the exception that the money was only lent for home mortgages, home improvements, and/or real estate development. The S&Ls didn't make business loans or consumer loans. And like a bank, if demand for mortgages was low, the S&L could pool the deposits and buy U.S. Treasury securities instead of extending loans. The interest earned on the Treasuries was used to pay interest to the depositors in the same way banks did.

The depositors actually owned the institutions, and profits were distributed to these *shareholders*. Recall George Bailey (played by Jimmy Stewart) in the classic movie *It's a Wonderful Life* and his travails at the "little old building and loan." A particular scene in the movie helps explain the S&L: George faces the depositors who'd lined up at the counter to withdraw their deposits.

George: No, but you . . . you . . . you're thinking of this place all wrong. As if I had the money back in a safe.

The, the money's not here.

Well, your money's in Joe's house . . . that's right next to yours. And in the Kennedy house, and Mrs. Macklin's house, and, and a hundred others.

Why, you're lending them the money to build, and then, they're going to pay it back to you as best they can.

Now what are you going to do? Foreclose on them?

Tom: I got two hundred and forty-two dollars in here and two hundred and forty-two dollars isn't going to break anybody.

George: Okay, Tom. All right. Here you are. You sign this. You'll get your money in sixty days.

Tom: Sixty days?

George: Well, now that's what you agreed to when you bought your shares.

George couldn't return deposits to the customers demanding their money because he'd lent it to their neighbors, who in turn had bought their homes and were repaying the loans over time. So there wasn't enough money in the Building & Loan to give all the depositors their money back, all at one time. Either George would have to call loans and force people to sell their homes in order to repay the withdrawing depositors or else he would have to raise new deposits to replace the funds of those withdrawing.

The primary difference between George Bailey's day and 1971 was that in the latter the federal government, via the Federal Savings and Loan Insurance Corporation (FSLIC), guaranteed deposits up to $40,000, so there was no, or at least less, fear that depositors would be scared into withdrawing their deposits in a "run on the bank." The S&Ls paid an annual insurance premium to FSLIC, just like the commercial banks paid premiums to the FDIC for insurance.

Securities Firms

People willing to forego federally insured deposits and accept some risk with their money could open an account at a securities/brokerage firm and become "investors" buying stocks and/or bonds instead of being merely "savers."

The income stream on that money was not from loans the firm made to institutions, and neither was it, nor the principal, government insured. The investors were *directly* participating in the "ownership" (stock) or "loanership" (bond) of the company, whose fortunes or misfortunes dictated the *return on* and *return of* principal. If the company for whatever reason failed to earn enough money, bondholders and stockholders might not get anything back.

Separated from commercial banks by the Glass–Steagall Act of 1933, securities firms did not take deposits to lend to borrowers. The Act's intent was to protect depositors from having their money lent to stock market speculators who might more easily fail to pay back the loans to the banks. The *source* and *reliability* of interest payments and the return of principal is the central question when lending money in the first place, whether depositing money in a bank or buying a bond. Also, banks underwriting stocks and bonds could lend money on easy terms to investors, thus helping to create demand for the very securities the banks were bringing to market and trying to sell to those investors.

A company borrowing money from depositors, via the bank, uses the funds in what it hopes will be a profitable enterprise, from which it promises to pay the interest and repay the principal. Loans to stock market speculators, whose "profits" evaporate if security prices fall, are a much riskier proposition and could in turn put the entire financial system at risk. Instead, such firms were conduits between investors providing capital and companies seeking it to build or expand their businesses, transferring risk in the process.

Through commercial banks and S&Ls, savers were *indirect* lenders to companies and consumers, using federally insured deposit accounts to channel the funds. Investors became *direct* "owners in" or "loaners to" the companies by purchasing the "securities" that the companies issued and securities firms "underwrote" and "distributed." That is, securities firms took the illiquid asset of a company and made it liquid by selling claims on its financial fortunes, effectively *securitizing* claims on the company's income stream by issuing stocks or bonds or both.

Even though securities firms do not take demand deposits, they are still subject to the vicissitudes of the short-term funding and fluctuating interest rates. In order to hold an inventory of stocks and bonds, either for selling to clients or as part of their own trading and investing, the firms pledge the securities on an overnight basis (sometimes up to several days) to borrow money from banks. The bank does not lend the full value of the securities, but instead an amount slightly less so as to protect itself from any adverse move in their prices. This so-called *haircut* in price varies depending on the firm's leverage and credit rating as well as the rating of the collateral securities being pledged.

This short-term financing leaves the securities firms with the same maturity mismatch problem that banks and S&Ls have. If for any reason the banks refuse to roll over the overnight loans or take a larger haircut due to a ratings change, the securities firms are forced to come up with more capital, sometimes by selling some of the securities in the inventory.

Transferring Risk

Following the trail of money through banks, S&Ls, and securities firms shows that Wall Street's business is to *transfer risk* from those who don't want it to those who do. As shown in Figure 1.1, selling stock to investors in an initial public offering is risk-transfer; so is underwriting the company's bonds.

The mix of a company's stock and bonds is the simplest example of what is called *creating tranches,* which rank investors' claims on the company's earnings and assets, as well as the risk characteristics according to security type. The document chartering the firm is folded in such a way that bondholders precede stockholders in a claim on the firm's income, with interest being paid before dividends. In the event of a bankruptcy, bondholders also have a prior claim to the assets of the company compared

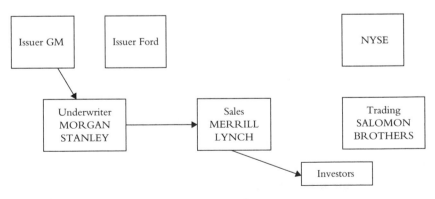

Figure 1.1   1960s Wall Street Primary Market

to shareholders. Broking shares and bonds previously brought to market is also an exercise in risk transfer, as shown in Figure 1.2.

Wall Street *connects and collects* in this risk-transfer business, bridging those with surplus capital to those with a deficit, exacting a toll for the service. It earns revenue by charging commissions and fees for transaction and advisory services related to the issuance, purchase, and sale of stocks, bonds, and insurance products, as well as from extracting bid/ask spreads and taking proprietary trading positions sometimes against those of its customers.

During the era of fixed commissions, the only access to these securities was through member firms of the country's stock exchanges, and the toll was high. In 1971, buying 100 shares of AT&T at $50 had a fixed commission of $440, or $4.40 a share. This put investors at an immediate 9 percent disadvantage on their purchase and another 9 percent on the sale. Today, investors can do the same transaction for about $8.50, or 8.5 *cents* a share. The SEC phased in competitive commission rates beginning in April 1971 and ending four years later.

The federal government didn't (and still doesn't) guarantee *funds* at a securities firm the way it had guaranteed them at banks and S&Ls since the 1930s. It wasn't until 1970 that Congress created the Securities

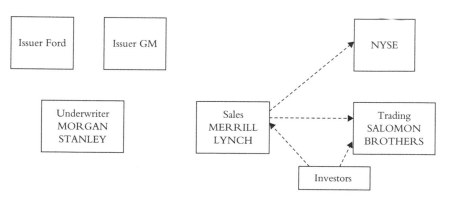

Figure 1.2   1960s Wall Street Secondary Market

Investor Protection Corporation, which was designed to be the investors' first line of defense in the event a brokerage firm failed and owed customers cash and securities missing from their accounts. The FDIC protected deposits at banks, and Congress wanted some protection for investors' money at securities firms. This is not a guarantee on the securities themselves, only the content of the accounts at the firms. But it is an insurance fund, not a federal government agency.

End of an Era

Harry Brown, the co-creator of the world's first money-market mutual fund, which opened to the public just weeks after Nixon severed the dollar's link to gold in 1971, died on August 11, 2008. He was 82. A month later, in the wake of the Lehman bankruptcy, his Reserve Primary Fund met its own demise: Tuesday, September 16, at 4:00 P.M., the Reserve Fund "broke the buck." Its net asset value fell below $1 a share. Shareholders clamored to exchange their shares for cash just like the mob had at George Bailey's Building & Loan in *It's a Wonderful Life*. Investors rushed to redeem their shares because the Reserve held $785 million in debt of Lehman Brothers Holdings Inc., which the day before had filed the largest bankruptcy ($639 billion) in U.S. history when weekend meetings with the Fed and the Treasury failed to secure a shotgun wedding akin to the one carried out between Bear Stearns Cos. and JPMorgan Chase & Co. six months earlier.

On Saturday, September 13, 2008, the U.S. Treasury and the Federal Reserve had summoned the chief executive officers of Wall Street firms for a second day of talks to find a solution to the plight of Lehman Brothers Holdings Inc. On September 14, Bank of America Corp. abandoned talks to buy Lehman Brothers Holdings Inc., less than three hours after Barclays Plc said it wouldn't buy the faltering investment bank, and instead agreed to buy Merrill Lynch.[5]

Fold Sides to Center

Within hours of the Reserve Fund suspending redemptions September 16, American International Group Inc, the biggest U.S. insurer, was effectively nationalized by the U.S. government with an $85 billion loan from the Federal Reserve in exchange for a 79.9 percent ownership interest in the company. Five days later, the two remaining bulge-bracket Wall Street investment banks, Goldman Sachs and Morgan Stanley, applied to the Federal Reserve for status as bank holding companies. The Fed approved the applications, which converted the investment banks into commercial banks subject to Fed regulation. The Wall Street business model had broken.

To grasp the magnitude of how things changed in September 2008, consider the following: Lehman, the oldest bulge-bracket securities firm on Wall Street, filed the biggest bankruptcy in history after Bank of America and Barclays Plc pulled out of talks to buy the New York–based investment bank. Bank of America, the biggest U.S. consumer bank, instead agreed to acquire Merrill Lynch, the biggest U.S. brokerage firm. Next, the oldest U.S. money-market fund, Reserve Primary Fund, broke the buck after writing off $785 million of debt issued by the bankrupt Lehman. The largest U.S. mortgage lenders and biggest U.S. corporate borrowers, Fannie Mae and Freddie Mac, had been taken over by the U.S. government the week before. IndyMac Bankcorp, the largest independent mortgage lender, had failed in August, and in the biggest bank failure in history, Washington Mutual, the country's largest S&L, filed for bankruptcy in late September, a month that marked the end of an era.

Chapter 2

Result, Turn Over

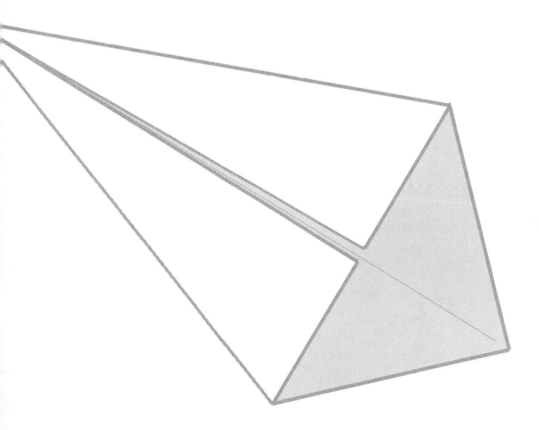

T he all-or-none proposition of Wall Street's risk-transfer products, owning stocks or bonds, didn't sit well with every investor. The stock could decline to zero, and the bond did not allow investors to participate in a rising value of the company. So Wall Street, for decades, worked with companies to offer hybrid securities that used Financial Origami to fold together the attributes of the hierarchy of claims on the company's earnings and assets. In effect, these instruments have some insurance-like traits that provide some risk management features. Issuers and investors share some of the risks of the securities. For example, *preferred stock* shares features of common stock and a bond. Like common stock, preferred shares do not have a first claim on the assets of the firm in the event of a bankruptcy. Like bonds, the shares have a fixed, periodic payment; common stock dividends are not compulsory as they are with preferred shares. *Convertible bonds* give investors the option of exchanging the initial loan into equity later if the stock price rises above a given price. *Convertible preferred stock* works in a similar manner. It's all simply a matter of Financial Origami, folding the attributes of a call option into a bond or preferred stock.

Companies also issue *callable bonds,* which grant the issuer the right to redeem the bonds before their stated maturity. An issuer has an incentive to do this if interest rates decline after the bonds are sold. For example, an issuer offers an above-market interest rate in exchange for the right to redeem the bonds before their stated maturity. The company would do this if interest rates fell far enough after the bond issue and would issue new bonds at the new, lower interest rate and use the proceeds to redeem the old, higher-interest bonds. The investor assumes the risk of early redemption and therefore demands a higher initial interest rate on the bonds. Companies also have issued *put-able bonds,* which allow the investor to sell the bonds back to the company at face value before the stated maturity date. Because this places risk on the company, it offers a lower initial interest rate than those without the option, and investors pay a price for that option in the form of a lower interest rate. In each case, there is a bit of Financial Origami. These are just a few examples of the risk management *features* folded together to create new securities. Thus a seesaw of risk transfer is developed between issuer and investor, trading portions of their respective risks in exchange for some price.

In addition to what *type* of securities investors bought, the *way* they bought them also offered a way to manage the risk assumed when purchasing the securities. Mutual funds *pooled resources* by issuing shares and using the proceeds to purchase assets (stocks). If any single security in the pool failed, at least it was not a total loss for the investors. This also made it easier for investors with small amounts of money to get exposure to stock market assets. The mutual fund was Financial Origami in that it presented a veneer product for investors who had too little money to invest in stocks directly. The same was true for T-bills, as in the case of Harry Brown's Reserve Primary Fund.

A money-market mutual fund is a special kind of company: It sells shares to investors and uses the proceeds to buy debt maturing in a relatively short time period that is also investment-grade as determined by the nationally recognized securities rating organizations. For decades the SEC only recognized Moody's, Standard & Poor's, and Fitch. The premise is that it's improbable that a highly rated company would default on its debt in that short a period of time, and a money fund breaking the buck seemed an improbable event. Aristotle, more than 2,000 years ago, labeled improbable events "Black Swans," a term that has come into vogue since 2007 with the publication of Nassim Talib's best-selling book *The Black Swan*. "Improbable," however, does not mean "impossible."

Hedge funds are Financial Origami of mutual funds. They are basically mutual funds for rich people, wherein investors forfeit a percentage of profits to the fund manager as an incentive, a practice prohibited in mutual funds. The typical compensation structure is for the hedge fund manager to get 2 percent of the assets managed plus 20 percent of any profits. Hedge funds are lightly regulated because the government reckons investors with more than $1 million to invest are sophisticated enough not to need the government looking after their investment decisions. The Securities and Exchange Commission has a similar policy for commercial paper, promissory notes issued by corporations. The Commission decided that large institutions investing in commercial paper didn't need its protection for short-term loans of up to 270 days, so those securities do not have to be registered with the SEC.

For decades, the *attributes* of securities as well as the *way* they were purchased were the main tools Wall Street offered investors as "insurance vehicles" to protect the value of their investments, to blunt the effects of adverse price movements. Harry Markowitz, a University of Chicago professor and eventual Nobel Laureate in economics, added to the risk management toolkit by showing how to *mix securities* in a portfolio rather than simply *mixing traits* in a single security or the way they were purchased. His seminal 14-page paper "Portfolio Selection"[1] showed how to optimize the tradeoff between risk and return by folding together a portfolio of securities based on how returns and their variance behaved in the past. Markowitz's key insight was that the expected return of a portfolio was an average of the past returns of the securities comprising it, but the risk, or expected variability of returns, was *not* a simple average. This was the "magic" of diversification and depended on how closely the securities' returns were correlated—that is, how often and to what degree the returns rose and fell together. The less correlated the better.

The Three Derivatives

Hybrid securities and diversification provided *some* degree of risk management, or insurance-like protection from adverse price change, but not enough to handle the volatile financial environment that would unfold when the government removed some of the strictures of the "fixed" landscape such as the peg between the dollar and gold and the ceiling on interest rates. Relaxing these government regulations incentivized Wall Street to trot out some old pieces of paper: options contracts, futures contracts, and swap contracts collectively known as derivative contracts.

Derivatives are *contracts,* promises to execute financial transactions in the future under specified circumstances, sometimes depending on whether specified events happen or fail to happen. They are *not securities*. The contracts are called *derivatives* because their price today is derived from the cash market price (today's price) and/or the likelihood of future *events* happening or not. These events could be rising or falling prices of securities, commodities, interest rate changes, as well as weather events or political races.

When pricing the savings account, one can ignore the source of interest being paid and principal being returned because federal deposit insurance guarantees it. Unlike the savings account, which can be valued by calculating the present value of the interest payments and the return of principal, pricing a derivative relies on the present value of securities or other derivatives, and often only if some event in the future happens. And the bank accounts are federally insured; derivatives are not, which makes the source of repayment in derivatives and the likelihood of events coming to pass all the more important.

Options

Option contracts are at least as old as ancient Greece, as reported in Aristotle's *Politics* around 335 BCE when Thales of Miletus used call options to profit in the olive-press market.[2] Additionally, Phoenician merchants sold options on the goods in their incoming ships. Options were even used in the seventeenth-century tulip mania in Holland.

Conceptually, options work like insurance, although technically they are not. Our health insurance premiums effectively give us *call options* in which we reserve the right to call upon the insurance company to pay our medical bills in a given year if they rise above a certain amount, the deductible. Our auto insurance is akin to *put options,* in which we pay annual premiums and reserve the right, in the event we total the car in an accident, to put the car to the insurance company and receive the blue book value in cash.

The year 1971, which would prove pivotal for many reasons, was seminally important for options. Professors Myron Scholes and Fisher Black wrote a paper on options pricing and presented it at a conference at the Massachusetts Institute of Technology in May that year. The options pricing model was refined with assistance from Robert H. Merton and published two years later as "The Pricing of Options and Corporate Liabilities." The Chicago Board Options Exchange opened that same year and provided the perfect testing ground for the practical implementation of the Black-Scholes and Merton model. Although the missing math Merton brought to the equation did come from rocket science (literally Ito calculus, for rocket trajectories), understanding the pricing principle is well within the grasp of those whose feet are firmly planted on the ground and who have bank accounts.

Within six months of its publication, the Black–Scholes model, as it is known, had become so widely used by traders at the CBOE that Texas Instruments produced a handheld calculator pre-programmed with the formula to generate option prices based on the model.

In his Nobel lecture, titled "Derivatives in a Dynamic Environment," Scholes told of his request to Texas Instruments for royalties. TI refused, citing the fact that the formula was in the public domain. "When I asked, at least, for a calculator, they suggested that I buy one. I never did."[3] Perhaps he should have. A year after winning the Nobel Prize in 1997, he and co-winner Robert Merton (Fisher Black had died a year earlier) helped blow up hedge fund Long-Term Capital Management using some of his theories, nearly triggering a U.S. financial market meltdown. The New York Federal Reserve arranged for 14 Wall Street firms, most counterparties to LTCM trades, to buy the troubled firm for $3.6 billion.

Futures

Futures contracts are at least as old as twelfth-century European trading fairs, which used the *lettre de faire,* a document specifying the delivery of goods at a later date. Because of the difficulties and expense of carting all of one's commodities to market, merchants would bring a sample of their goods to the fair and sell a *lettre* to the buyer. The goods would be delivered at an agreed-upon later date.

Initially used as a contractual agreement between two parties to exchange money for goods on a certain date in the future, at a price agreed upon today, these letters eventually were refolded to be negotiable and transferable. This enabled them to be sold to third parties, or even resold to fourth or fifth ones, before the agreed-upon date when the goods would be delivered at a specified location and sold to whoever held the *lettre.* The obligations, or risk, in the agreement could be *transferred* to another party simply by selling the document.

By the mid-nineteenth century, with a bit of Financial Origami, the letters had been folded into forward contracts known as "to-arrive" contracts. These are legally binding contracts in which a buyer and seller agreed to exchange goods for money on a specific future date. Futures traditionally were used in agriculture markets to manage the risk of price fluctuations between planting in the spring and harvesting in the fall. Farmers feared falling prices; grain processors feared rising prices. Ideally, the farmers could, at planting in the spring, contract directly with the likes of, say, Quaker Oats to deliver the harvested crop in the autumn but at a price negotiated in the spring. Geography and busy schedules make such direct contact expensive if not impossible, so the commodity exchanges developed to serve as a central market for placing orders and a clearinghouse for settling transactions, guaranteeing that trades will be completed if one party defaults. Farmers, traders, and companies willingly execute anonymous transactions because they know the exchange's clearinghouse itself is standing behind fulfillment of the obligations. Everyone entering a contract has to pay a security deposit. And each must maintain a minimum balance in that account, which is monitored on a daily basis to ensure that threshold is being met.

Swaps

The third category of derivatives is swaps, and they are as old as cave people. A swap is simple barter, an exchange of items deemed to be of equal value by the parties involved. As its name suggests, a swap means no money need change hands when entering the contract in the first place.

To see how swaps work, consider a simplistic example of two homeowners living next door to each other: They have identical houses and identical mortgages, except that one has a variable rate that resets every three months and the other is a fixed rate. Five years into their 30-year mortgages, the variable rate homeowner thinks, or fears, interest rates will rise and wants to refinance into a fixed rate mortgage. His neighbor thinks rates are going to decline and wants to refinance into a variable rate. But refinancing involves transaction costs such as title verification and closing fees. They could agree to make each other's mortgage payments. Alternatively, they could agree to calculate the prevailing fixed and variable rates applied to the outstanding balance of the mortgage (in this simplified example, the two mortgage balances are identical), net them out, and one neighbor will cut a check to the other for that amount.

With the most popular variety, an interest rate swap, two parties agree to exchange interest payments for a period of time, usually five years. One rate is usually *fixed* and the other floats, or resets, periodically during the term of the agreement. The floating rate is usually tied to an easily observable, transparent reference rate such as 90-day rates in London, the London Interbank Offered Rate (LIBOR). LIBOR is a time deposit of U.S. dollars in a bank outside the United States.

The interest rate swap contract answers the question: What five-year fixed interest rate delivers the same present value dollars in interest as five years' worth of the sequential 90-day rates currently available in the market? Remember, this present value pricing is the same as done with the bank accounts discussed earlier. Take the serial 90-day interest rates available in the market right now out to five years and calculate the present value of, say, a million dollars at those rates. Now, what fixed rate for five years would generate the same present value of dollars? That's the five-year swap rate.

The two interest rate choices are seen as identical because mathematically they are. That's why it's called a swap. Because the two are identical, no money need change hands when the contract is entered into. Every 90 days the prevailing 90-day interest rate is applied to the million dollars, the original fixed rate is applied to the same amount, and the net amount is given to the party whose terms are favored. In between these quarterly dates, in fact starting immediately after the contract is entered into, the contract changes value with changes in that series of short-term interest rates.

In some swaps, the parties exchange assets while others only exchange income streams. The variety of forms that swaps that can be folded into is almost endless, but they are all swaps. Credit default swaps, for example, instead of swapping interest payments, exchange (i.e., swap) the underlying assets (i.e., bonds and cash) being bet upon in the event of a downgrade or default or other so-called credit *event*. They are contracts, as opposed to securities. They provide protection against a company's defaulting on its debt. The contracts provide insurance-like traits, but technically are not "insurance." One party seeks loss protection and the other provides it, much the way auto and homeowners insurance policies work. In an insurance contract, an insurer pledges, against receipt of a premium(s), to compensate the insured for a loss, damage, or loss of expected advantage that the insured could suffer as a result of an *event*. Having exposure to a "potential loss," however, is not required in order to enter a derivatives contract. The contracts offer insurance-like protection, but need of

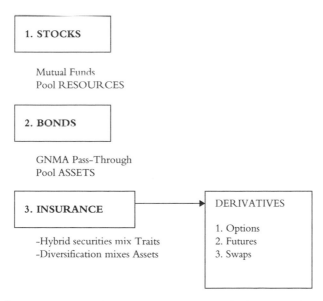

Figure 2.1 Wall Street's Three Pieces of Paper, Which Get Folded into New Securities

protection is not a prerequisite to enter one. Interest rate swaps protect against swings in the price of bonds due to changes in interest rates; credit default swaps offer protection against permanent impairment to the principal of the bond.

Figure 2.1 shows the basic pieces of paper that Wall Street traffics in when transferring risk from those who do not want it to those who do. It's the starting point for a series of diagrams to follow that show the evolution of Wall Street's Financial Origami.

Chapter 3

Fold Sides to Center, Again

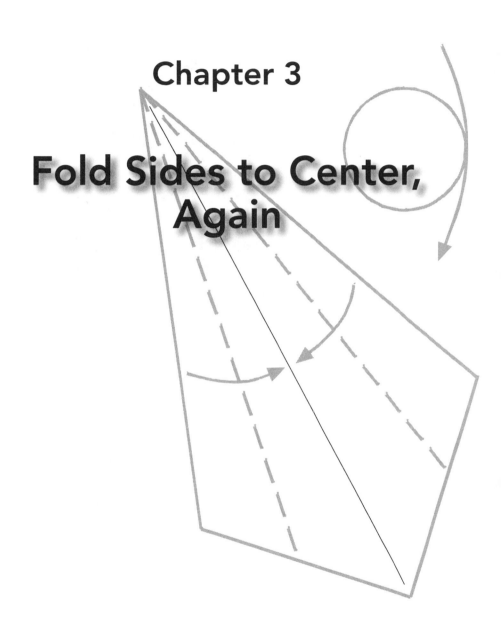

Terms such as *derivatives, exotic investments,* and *financial engineering* conjure complexity that can intimidate people not trained in finance, and sometimes even those who are. Despite the highfalutin language, Wall Street offers three easy-to-understand products: *ownership, loanership,* and *insurance,* stocks, bonds, and derivatives, respectively. It then folds and refolds them into more intricate investment instruments with higher commissions and wider bid–ask spreads, depending on incentives in a given situation. This is the reason for the metaphor of origami, which has a few basic folds used to create a large number of intricate forms.

For example, an equity call option folds together the features of a T-bill and a number of shares of the stock. As the stock price rises, the investor buys more shares; as it falls, shares are sold. This means buying shares high and selling them low, so there is a cost, or loss, by the time the expiration date arrives. That amount equals what the price of the call option should have been at inception.

An interest rate swap is simply a series of 90-day time deposits or futures contracts on Eurodollars folded into a single instrument. A trader or investor *could* create an interest rate swap from those futures contracts. Wall Street simply offers a veneer product behind which is the series of futures. An inverse floating-rate note folds a fixed-coupon bond with an interest rate swap. The list goes on. The "innovations" are really just new ways of packaging, or folding together, the features of the three basic pieces of paper. In other words, they are just Financial Origami.

The late Merton Miller, University of Chicago finance professor and 1990 Nobel Prize Laureate in economics, wrote that "The major impulses to successful innovations have come, I am saddened to say, from regulations and taxes."[1] Market participants try to avoid existing rules, regulations, and/ or taxes via "new" products or processes. For example, when the Clinton Administration passed legislation limiting to $1 million the amount of CEO/ officer pay that could be deducted as an expense, the officers demanded options as compensation. The options were not counted as "expenses," so they didn't reduce profits. If share prices fell, boards of directors often "reset" the price (exercise price) of options to compensate.

This should not come as a surprise, because people respond to incentives. Miller went on to say, "Each innovation that does its job successfully earns an immediate reward for its adopters in the form of tax money saved. The government is virtually subsidizing the process of financial innovation just as it subsidizes the development of new seeds and fertilizers, but with the important difference that in financial innovation the government's contribution is typically inadvertent."[2]

Incentives to innovate, however, are not confined to government-implemented *barriers* such as regulations, so-called *constraint-inclined innovation.* Relaxing standards or removing rules also can provide incentives. As we'll see, two of the biggest bursts of "financial innovation" coincided with the relaxation of rules, standard business practices, or regulations.

Whether it's the *existence, imposition,* or the *relaxation* of regulatory barriers, an initial phase of win-win for clients and innovators usually prevails because the incentives of the seller and buyer are aligned and transparent. These incentives lead to Financial Origami, which solves a problem. Wall Street, however, has a long history of taking a good idea and running it into the ground. The process can be described in this schematic: (1) Rules, (2) Refold, (3) Rave, (4) Ruin.

The rules or regulations in *stage one* can be in place, be imposed, or be relaxed. In *stage two,* responding to incentives from stage one, innovators refold the existing core or derivative products into new ones in order to solve a client problem or to skirt the rules or to take advantage of new standards, but in any event to make money. In *stage three,* everyone raves about the innovation's success. In *stage four,* what started as a good idea is taken too far and run into the ground.

Changing the Rules

Starting in 1946, when the Bretton Woods accord took effect just after WWII ended, the dollar-gold peg anchored the global financial system's trade and financial flows, and European currencies were pegged to the dollar within a narrow band of fluctuation. Foreign central banks could exchange paper dollars for gold, and vice versa, at a fixed price of $35 per ounce. And with the exception of a brief period in 1968 when the London Gold Pool broke, thanks to large French purchases, the official world price of gold was $35 U.S. per ounce.

After years of profligate U.S. government spending to pay for a foreign war in Vietnam and a domestic one on poverty in the 1960s, the *fixed* financial environment came under intense pressure in 1971. The U.S. government had been printing dollars to pay for these expensive ventures, and the surfeit of dollars created incentives for people, especially foreign central bankers, to exchange them for gold at the U.S. Treasury.

On August 15, 1971, President Richard Nixon slammed shut that gold window. The new environment of floating currency values unleashed a new risk: inflation that surged from 3.3 percent in 1971 to 12.3 percent three years later. The dollar buckled, and gold and crude oil soared as shown in Figure 3.1. U.S. Treasury Secretary John Connally in 1971 told

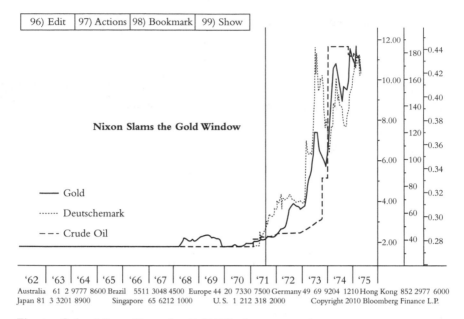

| 96) Edit | 97) Actions | 98) Bookmark | 99) Show |

Nixon Slams the Gold Window

—— Gold

······ Deutschemark

– – – Crude Oil

'62 | '63 | '64 | '65 | '66 | '67 | '68 | '69 | '70 | '71 | '72 | '73 | '74 | '75 |

Australia 61 2 9777 8600 Brazil 5511 3048 4500 Europe 44 20 7330 7500 Germany 49 69 9204 1210 Hong Kong 852 2977 6000
Japan 81 3 3201 8900   Singapore 65 6212 1000   U.S. 1 212 318 2000   Copyright 2010 Bloomberg Finance L.P.

Figure 3.1   Nixon Slams the Gold Window
Source: Bloomberg Financial, L.P.

a delegation of Europeans worried about exchange rate fluctuations that the dollar was "our currency, but your problem." Companies and investors needed new risk management tools to mitigate the risk of foreign exchange fluctuations and their attendant inflation.

Chairman of the Chicago Mercantile Exchange Leo Melamed asked University of Chicago professor Milton Friedman (another Nobel Laureate) to conduct a study on offering futures contracts on currencies. Published in 1971, the 11-page paper, titled "The Need for Futures Markets in Currencies," became the intellectual foundation for the birth of currency futures, which started trading six months later. Thus, the CME offered the first financial futures contracts, giving business and financial managers the same *risk transfer* abilities used in agriculture markets for more than 100 years.

Banks were limited to taking deposits and extending loans, and only in the state in which they were headquartered. That changed after 1981,

Fold Sides to Center, Again

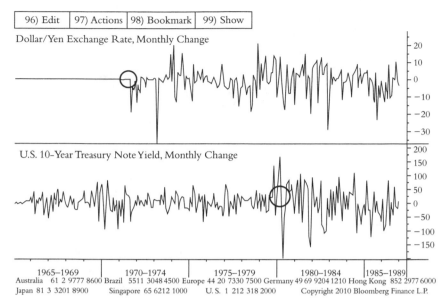

| 96) Edit | 97) Actions | 98) Bookmark | 99) Show |

Dollar/Yen Exchange Rate, Monthly Change

U.S. 10-Year Treasury Note Yield, Monthly Change

| 1965–1969 | 1970–1974 | 1975–1979 | 1980–1984 | 1985–1989 |

Australia 61 2 9777 8600 Brazil 5511 3048 4500 Europe 44 20 7330 7500 Germany 49 69 9204 1210 Hong Kong 852 2977 6000
Japan 81 3 3201 8900   Singapore 65 6212 1000   U. S. 1 212 318 2000   Copyright 2010 Bloomberg Finance L.P.

Figure 3.2 Exchange Rates and Interest Rates Set Free
Source: Bloomberg Financial, L.P.

the first full year the Depository Institutions Deregulation and Monetary Control Act (DIDMCA) was in effect with deregulated interest rates. The Federal Reserve had previously set interest rate ceilings in the banking system under Regulation Q, part of the Glass–Steagall Act of 1933.

The DIDMCA also expanded S&L powers, increased deposit insurance from $40,000 per account to $100,000, and allowed banks and S&Ls to pay interest on checking accounts. Citigroup lawyers, attentive to loopholes in the banking laws, that year moved the bank's credit card business to South Dakota to skirt usury laws.

The Act also allowed the establishment or acquisition of a trust company across state lines starting in October 1981, the same month that interest rates on 30-year U.S. Treasury bonds peaked at a record 15.84 percent. On October 1, 1981, within 24 hours of the peak in the Treasury yields, and therefore the trough in their prices, oil prices peaked and commodity trading firm Philips Brothers bought Salomon Brothers, as shown in

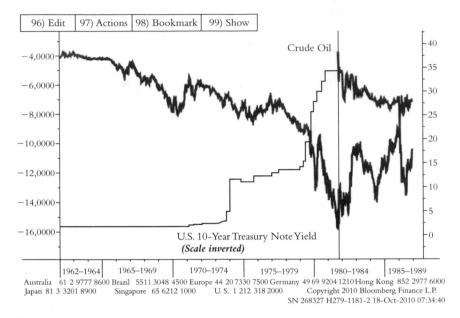

Figure 3.3   Oil and Bond Prices 1962–1986
SOURCE: Bloomberg Financial, L.P.

Figure 3.3. Oil prices, Phibro's area of expertise, were at a record high and bond prices; Salomon's area, at a record low.

By the end of 1981, U.S. Treasury-bill futures traded at the CME had become the biggest on the exchange by volume, trading 5.6 million contracts representing $5.6 trillion of securities. U.S. government debt outstanding at the time was only $820 billion and gross domestic product was $1.1 trillion. Basically, there were more side bets on T-bills than there were T-bills to settle the bets.

A New Environment

The new interest rate environment created incentives to develop risk management tools that would mitigate the impact of wildly fluctuating interest rates. In 1981, the Street refolded futures contracts to omit the requirement of physical delivery in this case, with Eurodollar futures, a contract on the LIBOR, helping it replace T-bills as the benchmark short-term interest rates.

Fold Sides to Center, Again

It was a wonderful piece of Financial Origami. For the first time, a futures contract settled *only* with cash, not with an underlying asset. This made it possible to bet on changes in the level or value of all sorts of indexes and events. Cash settlement opened avenues for index products of almost limitless variety. That same year, 1981, brought the first commodity exchange memberships for trading stock index futures, which also used the cash settlement feature.

Eurodollar futures enabled the widespread use of the third category of derivatives: swaps. The first interest rate swap was done in London in 1981. The first currency swap also took place in 1981, between IBM and the World Bank, and was a way to avoid regulations in place at the time: back-to-back loans, which were reciprocal agreements to lend money to each other's domestic subsidiaries. A British company would agree to lend pounds to an American company's U.K.-based subsidiary if an American company would lend dollars to the U.K. company's U.S.-based subsidiary. It worked, but it was a very messy process and time consuming to find eligible partners. IBM and the World Bank participated in the first currency swap by taking advantage of their respective, unique positions in the bond markets.

The World Bank had reached the limit of Swiss franc borrowing under Swiss law. IBM had a good reputation and willing buyers of its bonds, as long as they were denominated in francs. The workaround was for IBM to borrow in francs and for the World Bank to borrow in U.S. dollars. Next, IBM swapped the francs it had borrowed to the World Bank in exchange for the dollars it had borrowed. The two institutions deployed the capital and agreed to use those principal amounts to generate the interest that would be due on the bonds for the length of their life; that is, IBM paid the World Bank's dollar-denominated interest payments, and the World Bank paid IBM's franc-denominated ones. When the bonds matured, IBM returned the francs and the World Bank returned the dollars so that the principal payments could be made.

Wall Street responded to the changing regulatory environment after 1971 and 1981 with Financial Origami that refolded the ownership, loanership, and risk management products into new ones to help manage the increased risk in the new environment of volatile exchange rates and interest rates.

The money-market mutual fund took its shape from that of the stock mutual fund, which pools resources, buys a portfolio of assets, and then sells to investors shares of interest in those assets. Mortgage-backed securities (MBS) had a similar pattern. Banks pooled mortgages (assets) and sold them to a Special Purpose Entity (SPE), which in turn sold investors certificates representing claims to the cash flows of principal and interest payments, as shown in Figures 3.4 and 3.5.

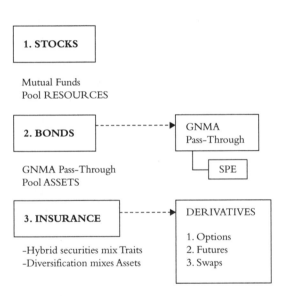

Figure 3.4   Wall Street's Risk Transfer Instruments

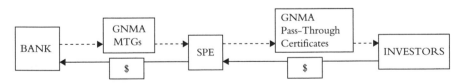

Figure 3.5   Government National Mortgage Association Pass through Certificates
SOURCE: Bloomberg Financial, L.P.

Investing in Mortgages

The reason for using the SPE was to comply with accounting rules to demonstrate that a "true sale" had taken place and that the mortgages were truly removed from the bank's balance sheet. While part of that was for accounting reasons, it was also to avoid any perceived conflict of interest. The bank was not allowed to meddle in the automatic process of "passing through" the interest or principal.

Securitizing mortgages enabled banks to tap investors rather than just savers. Banks channeling savings into mortgage loans could only offer as much of the latter as it gathered of the former. Moreover, the banks had to hold the mortgages until they were paid off. The SPE was set up specifically to carry out the pass-through task and got from investors the money to buy the mortgages, similar to the way mutual funds operate. Individual investors and institutional investors could now earn the interest rates previously available only to banks and S&Ls. And those institutions, having sold the loans to the SPE trust, had new funds to lend to new borrowers.

The first such securities were Government National Mortgage Association pass-through certificates, guaranteed by the "full faith and credit of the U.S. government." This made them as safe as U.S. Treasuries, but they had higher yields. The first GNMAs were as generic as could be: All the mortgages in the pool came from the same issuer (bank or S&L), had the same coupon, and were originated within three months of each other. Later patterns, as interest rates became more volatile, had a range of issuers and range of interest rates on the underlying collateral mortgages.

In 1971 Freddie Mac issued its first *participation certificate*, which mimicked the model of GMNAs using private mortgages. In 1981, Fannie Mae issued its first such security and called it a *mortgage-backed security.*

The federal government guarantees the repayment of principal and interest on all GNMAs. Every monthly mortgage payment pays some interest and repays some principal, so every pass-through payment gave investors some of their principal back. This also meant that if homeowners paid off their mortgages early, because they refinanced the mortgage or moved or simply had enough money to do so, the entire principal amount was returned to investors before the anticipated 30-year life of the mortgage pool. The risk of these securities is *when,* not *whether,* you'd get your money.

This so-called *prepayment risk* is a negative feature of mortgage-backed securities. Prepayment is a problem for insurance companies and pension funds, which tend to want bonds with longer-term maturities to match the longer-term dates on which they would have to pay out benefits. It is also a problem for smaller banks that might purchase the securities; they want shorter-term bonds that would match their shorter-term liabilities (deposits). The solution was simple enough, even if it took a long time for someone to light on it. In 1983, bankers applied to mortgages the principle of tranching from stock and bond issuance, as shown in Figure 3.6. That is, ranking claims on the income streams and assets of the company, Wall Street modified the pass-through nature of GNMAs and channeled principal payments, as well as any principal prepayments to one group of investors, buffeting another group from prepayment risk. Rather than pass through the payments untouched, Collateralized Mortgage Obligations (CMOs) tranched by channeling prepayments by maturity classes, as shown in Figure 3.7.

Whereas GNMA had an *explicit* U.S. government guarantee of payment of interest and principal, Fannie Mae and Freddie Mac had only an *implicit* one. The federal government promised a line of credit of $2.25 billion to each of the institutions if they experienced financial difficulties, but that was not the same thing as the "*full faith and credit*" guarantee of U.S. Treasuries. Investors knew the agency mortgages conformed to federal guidelines and were insured by the Federal Housing Authority (FHA) or the Veterans Administration (VA), but they were *not guaranteed* by the federal government.

Bankers soon realized that mortgages were not the only loans on their books that they could securitize. Loans and bonds banks held could be

Fold Sides to Center, Again

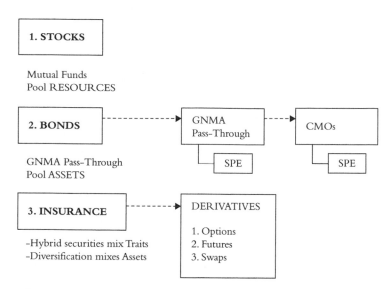

Figure 3.6 Collateralized Mortgage Obligations Used the Same Pattern as GNMAs
SOURCE: Bloomberg Financial, L.P.

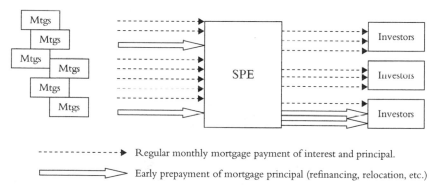

------------▶ Regular monthly mortgage payment of interest and principal.

⟹ Early prepayment of mortgage principal (refinancing, relocation, etc.)

Figure 3.7 CMOs Channel Principal Repayments to One Group of Investors Sequentially

folded together and sold much the way mortgages had been, as shown in Figure 3.8. The mortgages were insured; the loans and bonds being bundled were not. So the bankers added "credit enhancement" by purchasing insurance from a monoline insurance company, such as Ambac

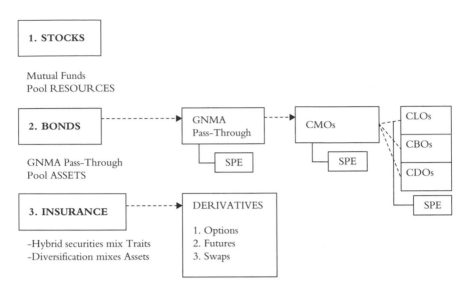

Figure 3.8 CLOs, CBOs, and CDOs Are Financial Origami of GNMAs

or MBIA. If the bond defaulted, the monoline would pay it off in full in exchange for the damaged bonds much the way an auto insurance company would "buy" a totaled car. The bank sold the "enhanced" loans to an SPE, which in turn issued and sold Collateralized Loan Obligations to investors. As before, this gave institutional investors access to yields previously only available to banks.

Banker Incentives

Bankers had several incentives for these activities. First, keeping the loans required setting aside regulatory capital to blunt any initial losses. The capital they set aside for these loans was dead capital, especially if the bank estimated the probability of loan default was low. If the loans were performing, the banks could entice investors to take the loans via CLOs, and the banks would free up capital to extend new loans. Second, accounting rules also allowed banks to recognize as revenue in the current year *all* the future years' servicing income, rather than spreading it out equally over the future years of the loan. Collateralized Loan Obligations resembled the original GNMAs, but differed in that *source* and *reliability* of the interest and principal repayments were not federally insured mortgages. Rather, the collateral was loans made to the banks' customers. Collateralized Bond Obligations simply packaged sovereign and/or corporate bonds. Collateralized Debt Obligations bundled all sorts of debt, including mortgages, sovereign bonds, and loans.

This is another example of Wall Street's being in the risk-transfer business; *moving* it from those who don't want it to those who do. While it does raise capital for companies and governments, that is a consequence of the task of transferring risk. *Initially,* it takes private companies public via *initial* public offerings. In doing so, risk of ownership is shifted to other parties. *Ownership* is not the only risk to transfer; so-called *loanership* too, via bond issues, transfers risk from those who don't want it to those who do. While government entities do not issue stock, they do transfer the risk of failing to collect sufficient tax receipts.

Wall Street firms also act as agents in the secondary market. After a security is sold to the public, if and when any of the buyers wants to sell the security, Wall Street can act as intermediary to find a willing buyer. It can also act as principal, "taking the other side of a trade or transaction" from a client or other Wall Street firm if a willing buyer cannot be readily found. In the secondary market, investors often move capital among asset classes variously seeking to assume more-risky assets or dispose of them.

Sometimes this means matching up buyers and sellers, in which case Wall Street is an *agent.* When matching parties are not to be found, the firms often step in to take the other side of the trade from their customers, as well as other firms on the street. This transfers the risk to itself, acting as a *principal.*

Insurance, the last category of Wall Street's offerings, historically was a *risk-sharing* business; losses in an insurance *pool* are split among the insurable group paying premiums. An insurance company that incurs large losses due to a natural disaster, for example, is allowed by its regulators to make up for the losses by raising premiums in the following years. Mutual funds pool investors' resources and issue shares in a company formed for the special purpose of buying shares in public companies. GNMAs pool assets of mortgages rather than pooling resources. Wall Street, however, introduced a new fold to the insurance process by adding *risk transfer* to the risk-sharing features. And it did the same with derivatives. When willing counterparties were not readily found for the firms to act as agents, they offered to stand in as principals and take the other side of the trade. The more they did this, the more the shape of the industry itself began to change.

Chapter 4

Fold Tip to Point

F olding existing products into "new" ones is not the only Financial Origami performed in the world of finance as the regulatory environment changed to fixed from floating for foreign exchange rates and interest rates. Wall Street also took on a new shape. It changed from a horizontal industry of firms specializing in specific tasks within the risk-transfer business into a vertically integrated one with firms assembling the respective tasks under the same roofs. In another bout of Financial Origami, the firms also refolded their business charters from private partnerships to publicly traded, shareholder-owned corporations.

Remember, Wall Street is in the business of *transferring risk*. Through advisory, it helps clients decide *whether* to do it; through underwriting, distribution, and trading, it helps clients decide *how* to do it.

Investment banking, advising corporate clients on mergers and acquisitions, financing, and underwriting sales of stocks and bonds was the near exclusive domain of so-called "white shoe" partnerships, such as Morgan Stanley, First Boston, and Dillon Read. They didn't sully their reputations with a sales force, much less a trading department. They advised their clients, using exclusive relationships, on transferring risk. When International Business Machines wanted to raise capital in the public securities markets, for example, it called "its" investment banker: Morgan Stanley. Companies usually had "exclusive relationships" with their bankers, who considered it bad form to try and poach clients from other Wall Street firms.

It was a clubby environment. Morgan Stanley was the preeminent investment bank in the United States after World War II. Like most, it insisted on being a client's-only investment banker. And investment banking was all Morgan Stanley did. The firm did not even have investment management, equities research, or government bond trading until that fateful year 1971. Brokerage firms, also known as wire houses, such as Merrill Lynch handled buy and sell orders from individual and institutional investors. For most of its history, Wall Street's "stockbrokers" were called "customers' men," and they were paid a salary, not commission. Trading firms, such as Salomon Brothers, dealt mostly with institutional clients such as insurance companies and pension funds wanting to acquire or offload large blocks (10,000 or more shares) of stock. The firms gradually began to encroach on each others' territory, creating a distribution channel housed under one roof.

As the Street folded into single firms the activities previously done by separate companies, conflicts of interest were inevitable. And they did appear in some *shape* or *form* over the decades: insider trading, front-running, price fixing, and others. But they reached epic proportions in 2000, and Biblical ones thereafter. Figures 4.1 and 4.2 show how Wall Street refolded itself from a relatively horizontal industry to a vertically integrated one over the years.

The vertical integration of the risk-transfer business created conflicts of interest, incentives for some employees to enrich themselves even if it meant favoring some customers at the expense of others. For example, when a brokerage firm in a syndicate has to take an allotment of securities, regardless of whether it wants to, there is an incentive to tout and cram that product through its sales distribution network. In this case, the corporate client selling the stock was favored over the retail client buying it. Similarly, investment bankers eager to win business from corporate clients

Fold Tip to Point

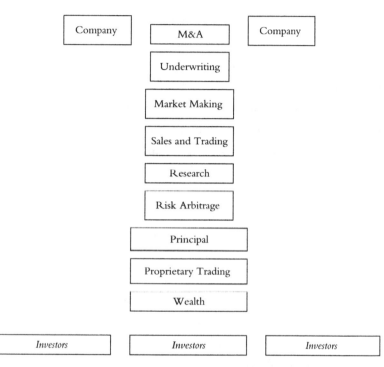

Issuer GM	Underwriter Morgan Stanley	Wirehouse Merrill Lynch	NYSE	Trading Salomon Brothers

Figure 4.1   Wall Street Historically Was a Relatively Horizontal Industry

Company   M&A   Company

Underwriting

Market Making

Sales and Trading

Research

Risk Arbitrage

Principal

Proprietary Trading

Wealth

Investors   Investors   Investors

Figure 4.2   Wall Street as a Vertically Integrated Industry of One-Stop Shopping

had an incentive to influence research analysts at the investment bank and give securities a favorable rating regardless of whether deserved. Having proprietary trading desks folded into the company alongside those filling orders for customers raised the prospect that the former could take advantage of the latter. Having the right to price securities or derivatives sold in the over-the-counter market and make mark-to-market collateral calls invites abuse.

People respond to incentives, and everything else is commentary. Money is perhaps the most universal of incentives, as it can be translated into whatever the individual actually desires. The *way* that Wall Street paid itself, maybe even more than the amount, goes a long way toward explaining its behavior over the years.

Other People's Money: Equity

Wall Street before 1971 was a guild of private partnerships that guarded their capital, used little leverage, and mostly limited their risk to trading blocks of stock for clients and shares of companies in mergers. The New York Stock Exchange prohibited member firms from being publicly owned. Partners accumulated capital in the partnership until death or retirement, at which time it was paid out. This also meant the partnership periodically needed to replace the "retiring" capital by bringing promising employees into the partnership.

"The partners at Lehman Brothers and the partners at Goldman Sachs and the partners at Morgan Stanley didn't take risk that was disproportionate to their resources, and when they did, they paid the consequences so they tried not to," according to Peter Solomon, a former Lehman executive and now the chairman of New York-based investment bank Peter J. Solomon Co.[1] The same is true for all Wall Street partnerships.

In relaxing the public ownership rule in 1971, the NYSE set in motion Financial Origami that would refold the Wall Street firms' corporate structures from private partnerships to publicly owned companies. Merrill Lynch went public in 1971 and got a new competitor the same year: discount broker Charles Schwab & Co. (founded as First Commander Corp.). Figure 4.3 is a timeline of when the bulge bracket firms went public.

The trend gathered momentum after the SEC abandoned its opposition to shelf registrations in 1981. Facing the challenges from commercial banks and other public companies with huge balance sheets, after the decision, the other large Wall Street firms also began to go public. This

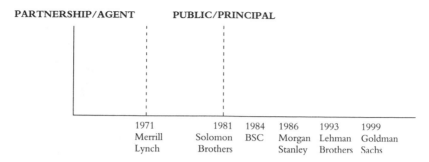

Figure 4.3 Wall Street Firms Go Public

allowed the partners to unlock the partnership capital that had for decades been pledged to the firms. In doing so, the firms could now rely on "other people's money" to run the companies. Merrill Lynch started the trend in 1971. Salomon Brothers, although not one of the bulge bracket firms, followed in 1981. The others went public subsequently.

After going public, the businesses exploded in size. For example, Figure 4.4 shows the surge in shareholder equity at Goldman Sachs from 1996, just before it went public, through 2009. "These firms are vastly bigger than they were, they're not privately owned partnerships any more that are filled with people worried about getting their own money back," according to Roy Smith, a finance professor at New York University's Stern School of Business and a former partner at Goldman Sachs.[2] After going public, however, Wall Street firms retained the general practice of paying the bulk of compensation through an annual bonus system, calculated from the top line of the income statement, not the bottom line. Typically, half of a firm's revenues were paid out in compensation.

People respond to incentives. "When the firms were private partnerships, you had to worry about how you were going to replace the capital" when a partner retired, says Anson Beard, who retired from Morgan Stanley in 1994 after 17 years at the New York-based company, where he ran the equities division and helped with the initial public offering in 1986.[3] "You think differently if you're paid in cash and not in ownership. It's heads you win, tails you don't lose. After we went public, we upped

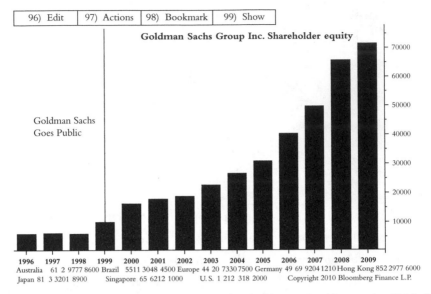

| 96) Edit | 97) Actions | 98) Bookmark | 99) Show |

Goldman Sachs Group Inc. Shareholder equity

Goldman Sachs
Goes Public

1996 1997 1998 1999 2000 2001 2002 2003 2004 2005 2006 2007 2008 2009
Australia 61 2 9777 8600 Brazil 5511 3048 4500 Europe 44 20 7330 7500 Germany 49 69 9204 1210 Hong Kong 852 2977 6000
Japan 81 3 3201 8900   Singapore 65 6212 1000   U. S. 1 212 318 2000   Copyright 2010 Bloomberg Finance L.P.

Figure 4.4 Goldman Sachs Group Inc. Shareholder Equity (thousands of U.S. $)
SOURCE: Bloomberg Financial, L.P.

the cash compensation dramatically." Merrill Lynch, the largest U.S. brokerage, even paid more to employees in 2007 than it collected in revenue. Revenue, net of interest expense, was $11.25 billion. Compensation was $15.903 billion, according to the firm's annual filing with the SEC.

"Shareholders share in the downside and not necessarily in the upside. That's the whole story," says John Gutfreund, who ran Salomon Brothers in the 1980s when it was renowned for the size of its trading bets. "It's OPM: Other People's Money."[4]

"We're essentially running all these investment banks and even the large universal banks on the same basis as if they were hedge funds," according to Smith, the former partner at Goldman. Executives "make big gains on any gains in the firm's income, whereas they're not exposed, they don't have to pay it back in the loss."[5]

"There are no partners of Merrill Lynch. There are employees," says Peter Solomon. "So they don't share in the losses and gains the way they should. They are able to shed those on to shareholders." These days, "shareholders and the customers are the people who are financing these guys," he said.[6]

Agents Transferring Risk Become Principals Taking It

The capital gained by refolding the business organization into public companies from partnerships complemented the firms' adding principal risk taking to the traditional relationship-based agents of risk-transfer function. The former needed a lot of capital; the latter needed less.

Wall Street's guild had been based on established relationships. Some corporate clients had been with *their* investment bank for more than 100 years. Being an investment banker was perceived as more prestigious than being a trader. The two leading Wall Street firms, First Boston Inc. and Morgan Stanley, honored a tradition dating back to J. Pierpont Morgan by treating traders as socially inferior to bankers. First Boston even called the offices of its underwriting business the "House of Lords" and the trading floor the "House of Commons." Trading was a bastion of firms such as Salomon Brothers and Goldman Sachs; it wasn't even a department at the white shoe firm of Morgan Stanley until 1971.

This coincided with the change in the rules fixing the value of the U.S. dollar to gold and with the SEC ordering the New York Stock Exchange to change its rules on fixed commissions for buying and selling stocks. It also coincided with the NYSE abandoning its rule prohibiting member firms from public ownership. Beginning that year, institutions could negotiate commission rates with their brokers. That same year, discount broker Charles Schwab opened its doors for business, Merrill Lynch went public (the first bulge bracket firm to do so), and Morgan Stanley added Mergers & Acquisitions, Sales & Trading, and Research to its advisory business.

It was the year the first money-market mutual fund, the Reserve Primary Fund, and the NASDAQ opened for business. It was also the year Intel Corp. marketed the first microprocessor, which in time would revolutionize the way Wall Street did business, from processing trades to extending mortgages and pricing securities.

Severing the dollar's fixed relationship with gold also triggered a surge of inflation, which leaped to a record 14.8 percent in March 1980, when it peaked the same month interest rates were deregulated, from 4.6 percent when Nixon broke the link. The Federal Reserve, whose job is to control inflation, appeared impotent. The rampant inflation was pushing interest rates on Treasuries above the ceiling on banks' certificates of deposits, which were set by the Fed.

The changes set in motion in 1971 were making Wall Street less clubby, more competitive. A seminal event, one that would help reshape Wall Street, occurred in October 1979. Salomon Brothers, in a most ungentlemanly act, snatched the largest corporate bond underwriting in history from Morgan Stanley. It was a two-part IBM bond issue totaling $1 billion, and Morgan Stanley, until that point in time, had been IBM's exclusive investment banker.

On October 4, 1979, Salomon Brothers and Merrill Lynch led 225 other firms in underwriting the offering. Salomon and Merrill were lead underwriters, each with $125 million. Morgan Stanley took $40 million; First Boston, $20 million; and Goldman Sachs $20 million. The trading houses and wire houses were overtly challenging the white shoe advisory firms. Solomon Brothers, specifically John Meriwether of LTCM fame, hedged the firm's position by selling T-bond futures.[7]

The event was all the more poignant because two days later Chairman of the Federal Reserve Paul Volcker unilaterally changed the rules of the monetary policy game in what became known as known as the Saturday Night Massacre. Forty years of Keynesian economics were tossed out the window. The Fed would no longer target a fixed overnight interest rate to combat inflation; instead, it would target money supply and let interest rates go where they will. And go they did.

On Monday morning, October 8, interest rates surged. The yield on 10-year U.S. Treasury note jumped to 9.83 percent from 9.60 percent on Friday, sending the price down. The IBM bonds were still "in syndicate," which means offered at the syndicate-selling price of $1,000 each from the week before. No one would pay that price, given the collapsing Treasury bond prices after Volcker's Massacre. By October 23, the 10-year T-note yield had rocketed to more than 11.00 percent. It wouldn't peak until 1981, at 15.84 percent as shown in Figure 4.5.

The trading firms were showing they were at least as well suited as advisers to manage the risk-transfer function in underwriting even if the firm did not have buyers lined up on the other side of the agent-based transaction. Relationships (bankers) were beginning to matter less, market savvy (traders) more.

Salomon had accelerated the Wall Street firms' move from being solely agents transferring risk to principals assuming it. Salomon was known for its trading prowess, putting its capital at risk to provide liquidity. Now it was putting the capital at risk for underwriting. Figure 4.6

Figure 4.5 Paul Volcker's Saturday Night Massacre
SOURCE: Bloomberg Financial, L.P.

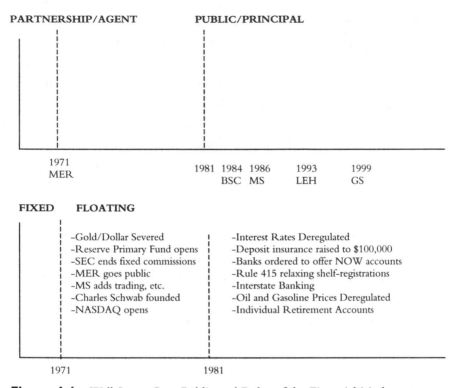

PARTNERSHIP/AGENT   **PUBLIC/PRINCIPAL**

1971   1981 1984 1986   1993   1999
MER   BSC   MS   LEH   GS

FIXED   FLOATING

-Gold/Dollar Severed   -Interest Rates Deregulated
-Reserve Primary Fund opens   -Deposit insurance raised to $100,000
-SEC ends fixed commissions   -Banks ordered to offer NOW accounts
-MER goes public   -Rule 415 relaxing shelf-registrations
-MS adds trading, etc.   -Interstate Banking
-Charles Schwab founded   -Oil and Gasoline Prices Deregulated
-NASDAQ opens   -Individual Retirement Accounts

1971   1981

Figure 4.6 Wall Street Goes Public and Rules of the Financial Market Environment Change

shows the timeline of Wall Street's bulge bracket firms going public lining up with the major changes in the rules for the financial markets.

Salomon would need both trading savvy and underwriting capital over the next two years as interest rates continued to rise until 1981, a year that brought the biggest changes in the macroeconomic rules since the dollar came off gold in 1971, not to mention the biggest change to the firm itself—it went public.

In 1981 the Securities and Exchange Commission relaxed its long-standing opposition to a rule prohibiting so-called *delayed offerings,* also known as *shelf registrations.* The Glass-Steagall Act prohibited commercial banks from underwriting securities; the SEC's new regulation, Rule 415, allowed them to sell securities if an investment bank had done all the underwriting paperwork first. The forms for a public offering could be filled out and the issue placed "on the shelf" for up to two years. In that interval, the company could go to market as conditions became favorable. Since the securities had already technically been underwritten, the SEC allowed commercial bank holding companies to participate in the distribution of the securities. That same year, the SEC changed its policy of prohibiting disclosure of a company's credit rating in prospectuses and other disclosure documents filed with the agency.

BankAmerica in 1981 announced plans to buy the discount brokerage firm Charles Schwab, founded in 1971 when commissions were deregulated. The rationale was that its captive audience of savers with bank accounts could be persuaded to do their investing in securities through the bank. Sears Roebuck & Co. thought the same thing about its captive customers and bought retail securities firm Dean Witter. Other rules relaxed that year would encourage this process. As one example, the 1981 Tax Act permitted individual retirement accounts, an incentive to *invest* rather than just *save* in banks or money market mutual funds. The increased competition from commercial banks helped accelerate the process of folding more of Wall Street's activities under one roof. More trading was one way the investment banks adapted to the competition. In order to trade as a principal, taking on positions that clients want to offload, a firm needs access to large amounts of capital so that it can buy and hold positions. Banks have this via their large deposit bases. Investment banks had only the partners' capital; there is no deposit base. So as the commercial banks encroached on the investment banks' trading arena, the investment banks needed more capital in order to compete.

In 1981 Goldman Sachs absorbed commodities firm J. Aron & Co., which mainly traded metals and coffee. The same year, Phibro Corporation, a commodities firm, bought Salomon Brothers, at the time considered *the* bond-trading firm. The Phibro–Salomon Inc. deal was done within 24 hours of the peak in oil prices and the trough in bond prices, as shown in Figure 4.7.

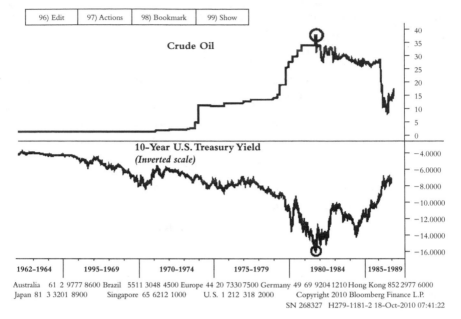

Figure 4.7 Crude Oil Peaked and Bond Prices Troughed on the Same Day in 1981
Source: Bloomberg Financial, L.P.

By April 15, 1986, the tables had turned. Crude oil futures had plunged 67 percent in a mere six months, to $10.20 a barrel from $31.70. Bonds were in favor; commodities, especially oil, were out of favor. During that same interval, 30-year U.S. Treasury bond prices soared to 104 from 76; yields fell to 7.12 percent from 11.40 percent. The same year, with bond prices high and oil prices low, Salomon regained control of the firm from the commodities arm Phibro and renamed it Salomon Inc. On tax day that year, the last day U.S. taxpayers could make contributions to Individual Retirement Accounts for the prior tax year, the rush into bonds helped drive prices up and yields down. The yield on 30-year Treasuries would not get that low again until 1993 and the onset of the worst 12-month performance in bonds in six decades.

Chapter 5

Fold Point Back

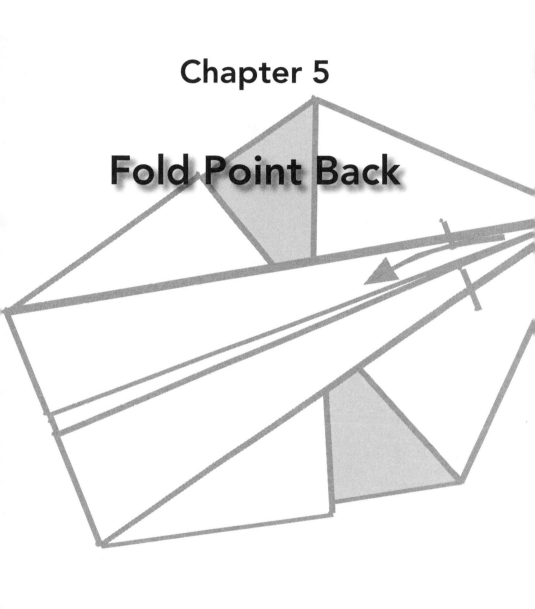

I n November 1999, Congress passed the Graham-Leach-Bliley Act, simultaneously repealing the Glass-Steagall-Act, which had barred banks, insurers, and securities underwriters/firms from entering one another's businesses ever since the Great Depression. The new law permitted commercial banks to engage fully in investment banking, and many started doing so. It also allowed investment banks to take deposits and enter commercial banking, if they were willing to become bank holding companies, which they were not, because of the increased federal regulation and scrutiny that would accompany such a move, so most did not.

Representative Jim Leach (D-Iowa) threw a party to celebrate the bill in the committee hearing rooms with ice cream, champagne, and a cake decorated with the words: "Glass-Steagall, R.I.P, 1933–1999." Federal Reserve Chairman Alan Greenspan, Treasury Secretary Lawrence Summers, committee members, aides, and lobbyists attended. Opponents said the bill lacked sufficient protections for consumers' financial privacy and would create gigantic new financial institutions that can engage in a new range of risky activities, escalating the threat of possible taxpayer bailouts. One in particular issued what turned out to be an eerily prescient warning. "Woe to the American people when they have to pick up the tab for one of the failures that is going to occur when profits disappear, prices shoot up, and misbehavior and unwise behavior takes place," said Representative John Dingell (D-Michigan)."[1]

The new law permitted banks, securities firms, and insurance companies to affiliate with one another, opening the way for financial supermarkets, and to compete head-to-head in the risk-transfer business. It was the final crease in folding the industry into one-stop shops for financial services, especially the commercial banks, which had been pushing into investment banking since 1981.

That same month, November 1999, Fed Chairman Alan Greenspan, U.S. Treasury Secretary Larry Summers, SEC Chairman Arthur Levitt, and CFTC Chairman William Rainer, collectively known as the President's Working Group on Financial Markets, recommended to Congress that it exempt over-the-counter swaps from regulation.

Two weeks later, John McCain made the famous campaign-trail comment about what he would do as president if Fed Chairman Alan Greenspan died: "I would not only reappoint Mr. Greenspan if Mr. Greenspan should happen to die, God forbid, I would do like we did in the movie *Weekend at Bernie's*. I'd prop him up and put a pair of dark glasses on him and keep him as long as we could." As he spoke, global stock market capitalization surpassed global gross domestic product for the first time in history.[2]

The stage was set. The Dow Jones Industrial Average peaked the next month, January 2000. The other major stock market indexes peaked in March, the same month a little-known economist, David X. Li, published a formula in a paper in the *Journal of Fixed Income* titled "On Default Correlation: A Copula Function Approach," as shown in Figure 5.1. Li would become famous for his formula; in time it would have as big an impact on financial markets as the Black-Scholes-Merton options pricing formula had in terms of *innovation* initially and *imploding* markets eventually.

Fold Point Back

The paper would in time become the academic study used to support Wall Street's turning subprime mortgage pools into AAA-rated securities. By the time it was over, the Street would create 64,000 AAA-rated securities, even though only 12 companies in the world had that rating.[3]

Whereas Scholes and Merton at LTCM had been betting on the convergence of price variables based on their correlations in the past, Li's formula was betting that past correlation would not change at all; that it would not deviate; that the past was indicative of the future. It would turn out not to be the case.

The ensuing bear market in stocks, from 2000–2002, curtailed investment banking business. From its peak in April 2000, the Wilshire 5000 Index, the broadest measure of U.S. shares, fell 48 percent by October 2002, the end of the bear market. The Standard & Poor's 500 Index declined the three consecutive years, the first such stretch in history, posting an average annual decline of 16 percent.

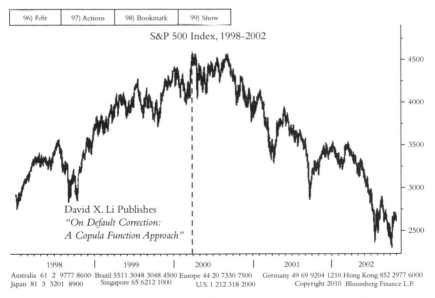

Figure 5.1 S&P 500 Index 2000–2002 Bear Market
SOURCE: Bloomberg Financial, L.P.

Chief executive officers of U.S. companies, confronted with a slow economy and a bear market in equities, cut back on stock sales and acquisitions. The value of stock underwriting arranged globally fell 43 percent in 2002 to $223.5 billion from $394.4 billion at its peak in 2000. U.S. corporate bond underwriting fell 21 percent to $641 billion from $814.2 billion in 2000. And the value of mergers and acquisitions arranged globally in 2002 declined 60 percent to $1.17 trillion from $2.91 trillion in 2000. At Goldman Sachs Group Inc., the number one arranger of mergers and stock sales, investment banking revenue shrank to $2.83 billion in 2002 from a record $5.37 billion in 2000.

Cracks had already formed in the Wall Street business model by 2001. New York Attorney General Eliot Spitzer sued 10 commercial banks and investment banks for inflating stock prices, using affiliated brokerage firms to give biased research and investment advice and "spin" IPOs of stock. Wall Street firms effectively had been using research as a sales tool for investment banking business rather than for the benefit of investors, breaching the so-called Chinese Wall designed to separate these functions and prevent conflicts of interest.

Rules, Refold, Rave, Ruin

Some in the investment banks succumbed to conflicts of interest and followed the pattern of *Rules, Refold, Rave, Ruin*. Wall Street has a penchant for taking a good idea and running it into the ground. It responds to the imposition or removal of a rule by refolding existing products into new ones, raves at initial positive results, and then ruins the idea by taking it too far and running it into the ground.

For decades, investment bankers had an unwritten rule requiring a company to have at least three years' profitability before they would underwrite its securities. The investment banks were lending their good names to the sale of an unknown company, and they understandably wanted evidence it was a viable enterprise. In the mid-1990s, the

Street gradually relaxed that rule, underwrote hundreds of dot-com IPOs, and collected the customary 7 percent fee on each deal. There is nothing wrong with IPOs or the commission structure per se, but what some firms on Wall Street did next epitomized running a good idea into the ground. One way to protect the securities firms' reputations when bringing public companies with no track record was to underprice the security, which almost ensured a soaring price on the first day of trading and sometimes for many days after.

By 1999 and the first quarter of 2000, investor demand for IPO shares had soared as new technology companies increased in value by as much as 698 percent on their first day of trading. VA Linux Systems Inc., a software company based in Fremont, California, increased to $239.25 from $30 on December 9, 1999—the same week John McCain delivered his *Weekend at Bernie's* comments praising Fed Chairman Alan Greenspan.

Given the demand for dot-com IPO stocks and given SEC regulations that prohibited underwriters from profiting from rising share prices in IPOs, the bankers responded to the incentives and held some shares back from the public. Then they preferentially distributed them to executives of favored or prospective clients in hopes of getting future investment banking business in return.

Barely one year into the post–Glass-Steagall environment, Wall Street firms were being charged with the conflicts of interest in their business model, perhaps nowhere more than at Citigroup, the commercial bank perhaps most responsible for the repeal of Glass-Steagall. Citicorp combined with the insurance giant Travelers Group in 1998, directly challenging the provisions of the Depression-era act that would die the next year. On December 20, 2002, New York Attorney General Eliot Spitzer, Securities and Exchange Commission Chairman Harvey L. Pitt, North American Securities Administrators Association President Christine Bruenn, NASD Chairman and CEO Robert Glauber, New York Stock Exchange Chairman Dick Grasso, and state securities regulators announced a historic settlement with the nation's top investment firms to resolve issues of conflict of interest. Citi paid the bulk ($400 million) of the $1.4 billion in fines. The "global settlement" concluded the joint investigation by regulators into the undue influence of investment banking interests on securities research. The SEC's press release said the settlement would bring about balanced reform in the industry and bolster confidence in the integrity of equity research.

A New Environment

The bear market in stocks following the bursting of the dot-com bubble in 2000 prompted the Fed to reduce its target for the Federal Funds Rate aggressively seven times in eight months and to 3.5 percent from 6.5 percent in an attempt to push the U.S. economy into faster growth. Within weeks of the 9/11 terrorist attacks, the Fed cut the rate to the lowest in the post-1971 dollar-gold peg era to counter their negative impact on the economy, and the U.S. Treasury suspended auctions of its 30-year bond, depriving investors of a supply of the most liquid, longest-dated AAA-rated debt security in the world.

The Treasury had been buying back some of its bonds during four years of federal budget surpluses, fiscal years 1998–2001. On October 31, 2001, the U.S. Treasury Department accidently posted to its Web site, about 20 minutes early, the decision to suspend auctions of its 30-year bond. They called it an "inadvertent" leak. In retrospect, it looks like an "inadvertent" decision altogether, given that surpluses were at that very moment turning to deficit again, which meant the Treasury was going to need to start financing those deficits. The long bond yield fell that day the most since the 1987 stock market crash. The suspension of 30-year bond auctions in 2001 intensified the debate about what fixed income securities institutional investors would, or could, buy to meet their long-term obligations. Insurance companies and pension funds, for example, are subject to investment policy restrictions limiting them to investment-grade holdings. Fewer Treasury bonds meant fewer alternatives.

Fold Point Back

The Fed's rate cut to a historic low occurred simultaneously to the U.S. economy's emerging from recession, although that wouldn't be made official until 19 months later when the National Bureau of Economic Research made its official pronouncement.

The recession of 2001 was unusual in several respects, chief among them that U.S. consumer spending did not decline, as shown in Figure 5.2. Every other recession since 1946 had been driven by a year-over-year decline in consumer spending, which comprises about two-thirds of U.S. GDP. This time, however, the business sector led the slowdown in the wake of its spending boom associated with preparing for Y2K millennium computer bug and Internet investments. The Fed, however, was busy doing what it too had done in every recession since 1946 (with the passage of the Employment Act, which gave the Fed the dual task of full employment and low inflation): cutting interest rates to stimulate the economy.

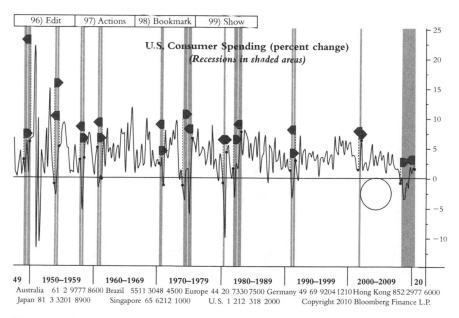

Figure 5.2 In the 2001 Recession, Consumer Spending Did Not Decline
SOURCE: Bloomberg Financial, L.P.

A New Risk

In 2002, the Fed cut its benchmark Fed Funds rate to a record low 1.25 percent, which helped send Treasury yields to historic lows and gave new meaning to the term "risk-free rate of return." This created problems for institutional investors such as insurance companies and pension funds, whose promised future payouts were based on a much higher interest rate environment, and money-market mutual funds, which began to use every basis point to differentiate themselves from the competition.

A new risk arose. Instead of the volatility in interest rates being the threat, now it was a subdued environment at record low interest rates. From the 1981 peak in interest rates through 2003, the yield on the benchmark 30-year U.S. Treasury Bond averaged 8.38 percent. Using the conventional decade time period, in the 1990s alone it was 7.00 percent (see Figure 5.3). During the economic expansion from 1991–2001,

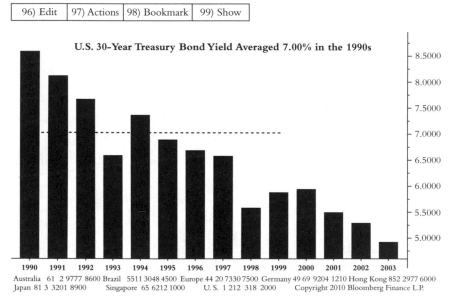

Figure 5.3 Average Annual Yields on 30-Year U.S. Treasury Bonds
SOURCE: Bloomberg Financial, L.P.

it averaged 7.50 percent. In the 12 months following the 2001 suspension of the bond auctions, the longest maturity Treasury-bond yield averaged only 5.35 percent, was never above 5.85 percent, and got as low as 4.16 percent. Through December 31, 2006, it averaged 4.98 percent. Investors developed a case of *yield reach,* trying to get a higher interest rate and seemingly ignoring the additional risk needed to get it.

The low interest rate environment created a "risk-free cash-flow crisis." For money-market mutual funds, every basis point began to count. Six-month Treasury-bill yields average 1.38 percent in 2002–2003, down from 5.15 percent in the 1990s. Commercial paper (270 day) averaged 1.53 percent in 2002–2003, down from 5.53 percent in the 1990s. This created incentives for money-market mutual fund managers to compete for every basis point, which in turn provided incentives to relax the standards on the quality of the commercial paper they would buy for the funds.

The historically low interest rates created a new risk for insurance companies and pension funds, which had calculated payouts based on the previous comparatively higher interest rate environment. The low-rate environment was a new risk, much the way volatility in currency exchange rates and interest rates introduced risk when they were set free. The low interest rate environment may have created problems for investors; it was a boon, however, for existing and potential homeowners, as Figure 5.4 shows; the value and volume of home sales surged. It also provided incentives for bankers on Wall Street to convert demand for mortgages into bonds for investors, especially given the increased transparency on interest rate policy from the Federal Reserve. On July 15, 2003, Fed Chairman Alan Greenspan sent a signal to the market that the central bank would maintain low interest rates for the foreseeable future: "In these circumstances, the committee believes that policy accommodation can be maintained for a considerable period." Two days later, the NBER said the U.S. economy had *emerged* from recession more than a year and a half earlier, in November 2001, the same date the NBER announced the economy was *in* recession. So a full 19 months after the recession ended, the Federal Reserve was pledging to keep

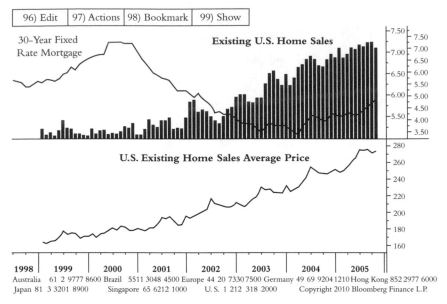

| 96) Edit | 97) Actions | 98) Bookmark | 99) Show |

Figure 5.4 Existing Home Sales and Average Price Rose as the 30-Year Fixed Rate Fell

SOURCE: Bloomberg Financial, L.P.

its benchmark lending rate low (unchanged) for a "considerable period." Figure 5.5 shows how low the Fed's target interest rate got and for how long the Fed kept it there during the recessions since 1971.

Every recession since 1946 swung to recovery driven by the housing sector, which in turn was responding to Fed-induced lower interest rates, shown in Figure 5.6. In the 2001 recession, consumer spending never contracted, as shown in Figure 5.2. The low interest rates over-stimulated an already expanding consumer sector and helped drive home prices higher. Mortgages with interest rates as low as 3 percent and house-price-appreciation running at 15 percent a year proved a powerful incentive for potential homebuyers, especially with the availability of mortgages with low so-called "teaser rates." These mortgages had low, fixed rates in the first two or three years but then reset to higher, variable rates for the remainder of the mortgage. In 2002, a record 6.4 million existing homes,

Fold Point Back

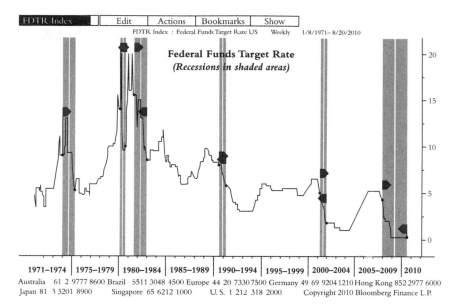

Figure 5.5 Fed Funds Target Rate and Business Cycle Dates, 1971–2010
Source: Bloomberg Financial, L.P.

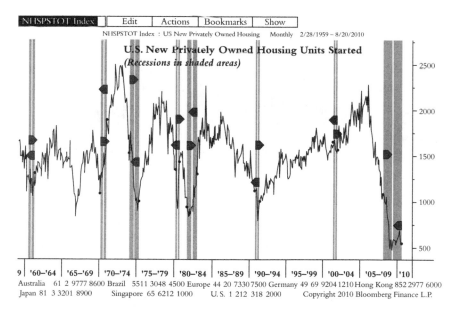

Figure 5.6 U.S. New Privately Owned Housing Units Started
Source: Bloomberg Financial, L.P.

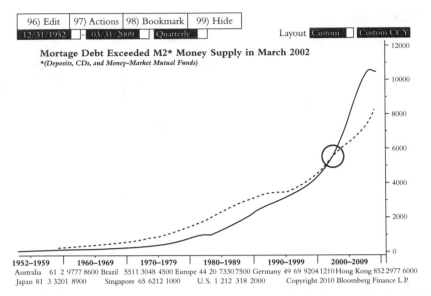

Figure 5.7 M2 Money Supply Surpassed Mortgage Debt Outstanding in 2002
SOURCE: Bloomberg Financial, L.P.

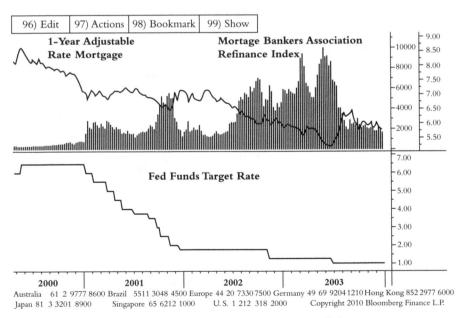

Figure 5.8: As the 1-Year Adjustable Mortgage Rate Fell, Mortgage Refinancing Soared
SOURCE: Bloomberg Financial, L.P.

including condos, sold in the United States at record prices, and mortgage debt rose above the U.S. money supply, as defined by M2 money supply: savings accounts, certificates of deposit, and money–market mutual funds shown in Figure 5.7. Imagine what would happen if enough homeowners tried to convert their homes into cash; it'd be the same as Jimmy Stewart's depositors all trying to get their cash at the same time: There was not enough money to go around.

Figure 5.8 shows homeowners refinanced their mortgages in record numbers, leaving investors in the original mortgage-backed securities flush with cash and facing a much lower interest rate environment in which to reinvest. Record high house prices, record rises therein, and record low interest rates would create powerful incentives in the mortgage market, the subject of the next chapter.

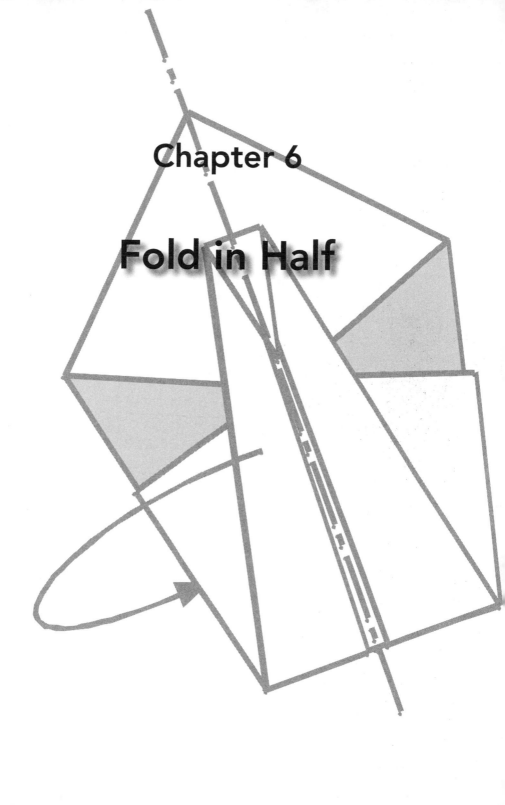

Chapter 6

Fold in Half

As the low interest rate environment persisted even long after the 2001 recession ended, investors began to reach for bonds with higher yields despite their attendant higher risk. GNMAs offered little yield advantage over U.S. Treasuries because both were backed by the "full faith and credit" of the United States. They were "explicitly" guaranteed. Agency bonds, such as Fannie Mae and Freddie Mac, offered as little as 20 basis points' premium over Treasuries because they were "implicitly" guaranteed; investors believed that if these agencies had trouble meeting their debt obligations, the U.S. government would step in and make good on those obligations. Investors would have to reach further afield to earn a higher interest rate.

Bank balance sheets also had mortgages that failed to conform to the criteria from the Government Sponsored Enterprises: a 20 percent down payment and less than a $217,000 mortgage at the time. These non-agency mortgages carried a higher interest rate because they were riskier subprime mortgages and *Alt-A* mortgages. Lacking any guarantee, explicit or implicit, Wall Street firms bought insurance on the mortgages from monoline insurance companies to give investors comfort when purchasing the bonds.

While Wall Street folded into single firms all the services previously provided by separate companies, it performed Financial Origami on the mortgage-lending process by unfolding the mortgage market. Here's how. For decades banks and S&Ls performed all three functions—funding, originating, and servicing of mortgages—and kept the mortgages until they were paid off just like Jimmy Stewart's Building & Loan had. Homeowners made monthly payments, and the financial institutions used the funds to pay depositors interest and repay their principal. Advances in computerized credit scoring models, helped by the microprocessor first marketed to the public in that pivotal year 1971, enabled Wall Street to unfold the mortgage process so that the three steps were carried out by different types of firms specializing in one of the processes. Banks outsourced to mortgage brokers the task of getting people to borrow for homes and gave loans to the future homebuyers. Securities firms focused on bundling that pipeline of mortgages and selling them to investors.

Mortgage Origami

Banks had been bundling government-guaranteed mortgages into securities and selling them to investors as GNMA pass-through securities since 1970. In the 1983, Wall Street refolded that product's pattern into CMOs. The payments on these government-agency-backed mortgages were not *explicitly* guaranteed by the government, and the bonds were designed to unbundle the risk of any prepayments by channeling them to one class of bondholder (short-term) until they were paid off before routing prepayments to the more-protected tranche.

Unfolding the mortgage process provided commercial and investment bankers with incentives to create loans they previously might never have made and some of which were not the best of quality and did not conform to the standards set by Fannie Mae and Freddie Mac. Mortgage bankers and brokers increasingly borrowed money and in turn lent to potential homebuyers, but doing so with the explicit intent of selling those mortgages to Wall Street for packaging.

The risk of these types of loans, in the so-called originate-to-distribute model, was not *prepayment,* as with GNMAs and CMOs, but *nonpayment.* Borrowers might, for whatever reason, fail to make timely payments of interest and principal on their mortgages. Bundling these types of loans would be different from bundling those that the federal government guaranteed either *explicitly* or *implicitly.* Lacking such guarantees, these asset bundles were riskier, like corporate equity and debt were risky. So instead of tranching by maturity, Wall Street tranched by credit risk, the way a company tranches its credit risk in its capital structure. As with companies, some investors had first claim on the *income* stream and were the last to suffer bankruptcy losses. Other investors had the last claim on income and were the first to suffer bankruptcy losses, as shown in Figure 6.1.

A firm's stakeholder ranking of claims on income and assets in the event of default is the inverse of its obligation to absorb losses. Senior bondholders have first claim on income, to get their interest payments, and first claim on assets in the event of default or bankruptcy. Subordinated bondholders are next in line, then preferred shareholders, and then equity holders last. So it was a simple matter of Financial Origami to bundle the riskier, non-guaranteed assets on bank balance sheets and create "mini companies." Collateralized Loan Obligations bundled *loans* instead of *mortgages;* Collateralized Bond Obligations did the same with pools of *bonds.* Collateralized Debt Obligations used mixtures of all sorts of *debt*: loans, bonds, and/or mortgages. Effectively, CDOs, CLOs, and CBOs are "little companies" (i.e., SPEs) whose only assets are the loans or bonds that banks want to remove from their balance sheets or bought in the open market to fill the SPE. These companies sell senior, subordinated (or mezzanine), and equity tranches to investors, just like other companies sell such tranches of bonds. In each such firm, the first defaults would be channeled initially to the equity tranche, the same as with a regular

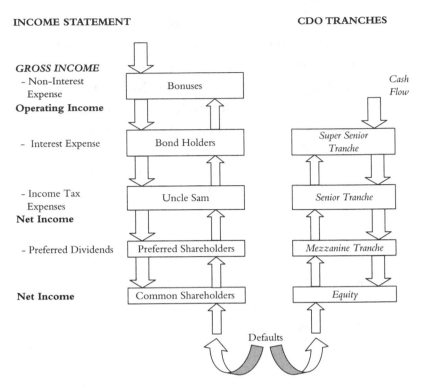

INCOME STATEMENT

CDO TRANCHES

Figure 6.1   The Cash Flows and Default Flows for CDOs Are the Same as for Companies

company. The subordinated tranche absorbed the next round of losses until that capital is wiped out. And the senior tranche would be the last in line to be hit with defaults, if they ever were enough to wipe out the lower tranches. The most senior tranches are the first to receive cash flows and are protected against default until the more junior tranches are depleted. But how likely was default? As long as people, or most of them anyway, paid their mortgages, there was no problem.

Collateralized debt obligations made from mortgages were folded so that the lower-rated tranches absorbed defaults until their capital was depleted, at which point the next higher-rated tranche began absorbing defaults and so on. The AAA-rated securities at the top of the securitization chain were so rated only because the lower tranches absorbed early defaults and acted as a sort of insurance policy against the senior tranche being affected by defaults. To have created the AAA-rated group in the first place, rating agencies needed to ascertain the likelihood that many borrowers would default at the same time. The rating agencies and Wall Street turned to the *copulas* formula that economist David X. Li first trotted out the month the major stock market indexes topped in 2000. What was the probability of serial, or even simultaneous, defaults? To answer that question, we need to return to 1971 again: the Black-Scholes option pricing model and the computational power of the microchip.

Subprime Origami

Little recognized but central to understanding how mortgages work and the nexus of how they touched off the financial crisis is the embedded option in all mortgages. Inside a conventional mortgage, one that conforms to GSE standards, or a so-called prime mortgage, is the *right* to pay off the loan early, to *prepay* the mortgage. This is a *call option* on the mortgage, and it is free in the sense that there is no penalty for exercising the option to prepay. This enables homeowners to refinance their loans at a lower interest rate if rates decline after they take out the mortgage. They also have a *put option* in that they can walk away from the mortgage for any reason: loss of job, death of the breadwinner, or other such event. This means they can *put* the house to the lending institution.

It was only a slight origami wrinkle in the paper to apply this to subprime mortgages. Because these borrowers were not prime credits and often failed to meet the down payment requirement of the GSEs, banks and other lending companies developed so-called *hybrid mortgages* that had a fixed rate for a few years (usually two or three) and then switched to an adjustable rate, starting at a much higher interest rate and resetting every six months to market rates for the remainder of the 30 years (2/28 and 3/27 were the most common). Given that banks (and the GSEs) were under pressure from Congress, via the Community Reinvestment Act, to lend to lower-income families, the banks refolded the mortgage option so that *they* had the right to call the loan in an unconventional way. Here's how.

House prices in the United States were rising as much as 15 percent a year on a national average from 2000 to 2006, compared with an average closer to 6 percent in previous years. Subprime borrowers would build equity in the house with hybrid mortgages as prices rose for two or three years, at which time they could refinance the loan, perhaps into a conventional conforming (prime) loan, because they now had some equity in the house. In order to prevent, or at least discourage, homeowners from taking that equity out of the house as it was accumulating, banks imposed prepayment penalties on subprime borrowers. High enough penalties secured a call option for the lender *not* to renew the loan at the end of the two or three years, if the house price failed to rise enough to give the owner GSE-threshold equity. If home prices failed to rise, the homeowner would not have accrued any equity and the lender would not agree to refinance the loan. The borrower effectively lost the right to prepay (call option), although retaining the right to default (put option). As the nexus for how the subprime crisis became the financial crisis, later we'll examine how this mechanism is similar Wall Street's own funding model.

The Rating Game

In 1971 Harry Brown's Reserve Primary Fund got started by passing on to investors some of the government-guaranteed interest from T-bills held in the fund, retaining some money to run his company. The result was effectively an AAA-rated security. A little Financial Origami created GNMA pass-through securities, which channeled *explicitly* government-guaranteed monthly mortgage payments to investors, retaining a small servicing fee: AAA-rated security. A bit of refolding and CMO structures funneled to investors the monthly payments from *implicitly* government-guaranteed mortgages, using tranches to channel any prepayments to those lower on the pecking order: AAA-rated security. With GNMAs, each investor received payments of interest and principal. In CMOs some investors were "senior" to others in that the subordinate classes absorbed the prepayment of principal, insulating the senior class until the subordinate class(es) were completely paid back.

Could CDOs containing subprime mortgages, high-cost mortgages for people with poor credit history and or little money as a down payment, with tranches that channeled any *defaults* to the investors lower in the pecking order and ostensibly insulating the higher ranked investors from losses produce a AAA-rated security? That would depend on the rating agencies.

Recall that in addition to long-term borrowing, companies take out short-term loans via the commercial paper market. Figure 6.2 shows that Wall Street used the same pattern to create so-called Structured Investment Vehicles (SIVs), which were special-purpose entities that

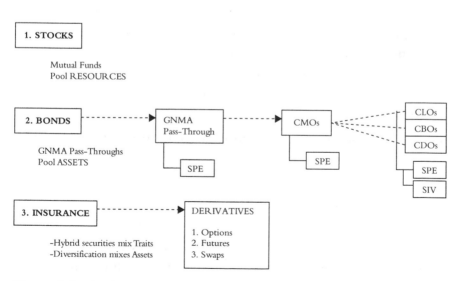

Figure 6.2 Credit Derivatives Follow the Same Pattern as GNMAs and CMOs

issued short-term debt via commercial paper promissory notes from the "little companies" and used the proceeds to buy assets from the bank's balance sheet or other debt securities from the open market. This is another example of taking a good idea and running it into the ground. When the commercial paper matured, the SIV would borrow again in the commercial paper market to repay the maturing short-term loans. Often, the same investors would re-lend to the SIV over and over and over again. If they, or any investors, refused to lend to the SIVs at rollover time, the SIV might have to sell its assets, putting downward pressure on prices. Withholding the funds from the SIVs was akin to Jimmy Stewart's depositors withdrawing their money from the Building & Loan. When investors balked at rolling over their loans to the SIVs, the banks took the assets previously sold to the SIV back onto their own books. So, the original transaction did not turn out to be a "true sale" after all.

Because the bonds had no *guarantee,* explicit or implicit, for timely payment of interest and principal, issuers often paid monoline insurance companies to insure the cash flow payments so that investors would feel comfortable buying them. So not only was Wall Street manufacturing product, loans that would not have otherwise been extended, it was also manufacturing their bundled byproduct in the form of the mini companies.

Companies manufacture products that often get rated by objective, third-party companies so potential buyers have information for their purchasing decisions. *Consumer Reports,* for example, rates toasters and other household appliances. And J.D. Powers rates cars, dryers, and refrigerators, among other products. The manufacturers do not initiate the process; the raters take it upon themselves. The manufacturers do not pay the raters to perform these product evaluations; to do so would be a conflict of interest. Consumers would be suspicious of the rating, the way a favorable clinical test of a new drug paid for by the drug manufacturer would be. Wall Street, however, does it differently. The company whose product is under review requests and pays for a report on its creditworthiness.

Fold in Half

The mini companies *paid* the agencies for the credit rating and then used it to convince creditors to loan money. Investors used the ratings to make decisions on purchases and sales of the securities. Ratings on a company's bonds impact its borrowing costs as well as the pool of potential investors permitted to buy its debt. The Securities and Exchange Commission allows financial firms to use the ratings for regulatory purposes; this includes calculating regulatory capital, or dead capital. Most, if not all, insurance companies' and pension funds' investment policy constraints require them to hold only investment-grade issues. Money-market mutual funds have similar constraints. And if a security in the portfolio loses that coveted status of investment grade, the bond must be sold.

Rating the bonds of a company, which can alter strategy or sell assets to increase its cash flow and enhance its ability to service its debt, is one thing. Rating CDOs, which do not have the choices open to conventional companies to improve cash flow, is something else altogether. Recall that in January 2008 only 12 companies in the world were AAA rated, yet *64,000 structured products* were. CDOs, however, were not company debt in the conventional sense. Company securities were not being rated. Rather, CDOs *mimicked* the capital structure of a company that issued debt securities and then paid the rating agencies to rate the securities. To ensure the "investment grade" rating for a large portion of the CDO, Wall Street firms consulted with the rating agencies during the structuring.[1] That is a clear conflict of interest. In charge of the manufacturing process, Wall Street firms could modify the structure of the CDO to make sure the rating met the grade for investors whose investment policies required that any fixed income securities they bought were investment grade.

Investors already had a case of yield reach, but they were unlikely and/or unable to invest in subprime mortgages. And most institutions' investment policy committee guidelines prohibit owning securities lower than investment grade. Wall Street needed to offer products that met these guidelines, which meant high-grade bonds, as rated by, at the time, only three nationally recognized statistical rating organizations (NRSROs) as designated by the SEC.

The SEC provided an aura of validation for rating companies by allowing financial firms to use their ratings for regulatory purposes. Institutions that owned AAA-rated bonds had to set aside a smaller amount of regulatory capital as a buffer against losses, which provided an incentive for Wall Street to offer AAA-rated bonds. When Moody's and Standard & Poor's assigned AAA ratings to securities created from subprime mortgages, investors took it as the equivalent of an SEC seal of approval.

Banker Incentives

Bankers had at least three incentives for unfolding the mortgage process. First, holding mortgages while homeowners paid them off tied up capital and prevented banks from taking advantage of any other opportunities that might arise. Packaging and selling the loans and collecting the servicing fees addressed that. Second, the loans might require a larger regulatory capital reserve set aside (dead capital) if held separately, compared to what's required if bundled into an AAA-rated CDO. The amount of dead capital to set aside is a function of the rating of the debt; the higher the rating, the less dead capital. So converting loans into AAA-rated securities and holding them instead of the raw material of loans made perfect sense. Third, banks could report in the current year *all* the revenue they would receive from servicing the mortgages for the entire life of the loans, in some cases as long as 30 years. People respond to incentives, and bankers are people too.

Commercial banks and investment banks alike offered to securitize and sell almost any home loans that mortgage brokers brought for packaging. And make loans they did, as Figure 6.3 shows. This relaxed previous standards under which the packaging banks' mortgage loans had endured a more rigorous process at inception. The lax standards gave *securitization* a bad name in the process.

Fold in Half

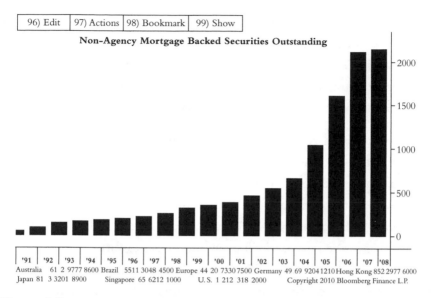

Figure 6.3 Non-Agency MBS Surged after 2002 (billions of U.S. $)
SOURCE: Bloomberg Financial, L.P.

There is nothing wrong with securitization; it's the Financial Origami that Wall Street uses to transfer the risk of private ownership of a company to public shareholders. The shares document evidence of ownership claims to the company's income stream. Securitization is also how banks take the risk of holding mortgages to maturity and transfer it to investors willing to assume that risk and receive the generally higher returns. Recall, investors previously had no way to earn returns from these assets; only banks and S&Ls were allowed to extend real estate loans.

The mortgage market episode of Financial Origami followed the familiar pattern of rules, refold, rave, and ruin. The Street relaxed its standards for granting mortgages, refolded the mortgage backed securities product to permit low-doc (low documentation) and ninja (no income, job or assets) loans, and eventually ran a good idea, mortgage securitization, into the ground.

Few banks did more to bring us the subprime mortgage debacle than Europe's biggest. London-based HSBC's 2003 purchase of Illinois-based Household International added almost 50 million U.S. clients, many with poor credit histories. The deal brought legitimacy to a business few considered respectable. HSBC would eventually signal the onset of the subprime crisis when it announced bigger than expected losses from such mortgages in February 2007. Fed Chairman Ben Bernanke described the mortgage expansion process this way in testimony before the Committee on Financial Services, U.S. House of Representatives, September 20, 2007.

> The expansion was fueled by innovations—including the development of credit scoring—that made it easier for lenders to assess and price risks. In addition, *regulatory changes* and the ongoing growth of the secondary mortgage market increased the ability of lenders, who once typically held mortgages on their books until the loans were repaid, to sell many mortgages to various intermediaries, or "securitizers." The securitizers, in turn, pooled large numbers of mortgages and sold the rights to the resulting cash flows to investors, often as components of structured securities. This "originate-to-distribute" model gave lenders (and, thus, mortgage borrowers) greater access to capital markets, lowered transaction costs, and allowed risk to be shared more widely. The resulting increase in the supply of mortgage credit likely contributed to the rise in the homeownership rate from 64 percent in 1994 to about 68 percent now (see Figure 6.4), with minority households and households from lower-income census tracts recording some of the largest gains in percentage terms.

Bear in mind CDOs (a special case is discussed later) and family members CLOs and CBOs are *securities*. They have underlying assets generating a stream of income in the form of interest and principal payments by borrowers, provided they made their scheduled payments. Via Financial Origami, Wall Street bankers simply pooled those assets and sold certificates representing a legal claim on those income streams. If homeowners defaulted, the CDO investors would stop receiving that stream and would wind up owning the impaired, underlying asset. When the CDO trustee sold the property perhaps at 80 cents or 70 cents on the dollar, for

Fold in Half

Figure 6.4   Percent of U.S. Population Owning Home; Percent Employed

example, the investors would receive that payment rather than the 100 cents in the case of guaranteed bonds.

Manufactured Product

Effectively, Wall Street bankers had manufactured from subprime mortgages a "new" product that hadn't existed before: the CDO structure that ratings agencies approved worthy of AAA-rated status.

Financial Origami of products had produced ways for businesses, investors, and traders to blunt the effects of adverse price movements in currencies, interest rates, and commodities via futures contracts on exchanges as well as forward contracts in the over-the-counter market. But there was nothing to insulate market participants from a complete loss of principal due to default or bankruptcy. If Wall Street firms could refold its pieces of paper and offer a "new" product with that feature, it'd have something else to sell to clients.

The bankers, motivated by such an incentive, did it via a derivative, a contract involving a financial transaction(s) in the future if a specific event(s) occurs. The newly folded piece of paper was called a *credit default swap*. The banks with loans or bonds made annual payments to a third party who promised to buy the securities at 100 cents on the dollar if a "credit event" happened. This is similar to insurance but technically is not, and nor is it regulated as such. It's akin to a put option that lets the bankers "put" the loans or bonds to the third party in exchange for their face value.

Wall Street bankers used credit default swaps as a means for banks to transfer the default risk of a portfolio of commercial loans to investors who were willing to take risk, freeing up bank regulatory capital in the process. A bank entering into a CDS contract shifted the risk of default to a third party. From the bankers' perspective, U.S. accounting rules considered such loans "protected" and therefore required that no regulatory capital (i.e., dead capital) needed to be set aside.

As with most "new" products Wall Street bankers have devised over the years, CDS served a beneficial role when first introduced. But as we've seen, Wall Street has a penchant for taking a good idea and running it into the ground. As we'll see in the next chapter, credit default swaps were no different in this regard, and what had started as a piece of paper that transferred risk became one that manufactured it.

Chapter 7

Pull Neck Upright

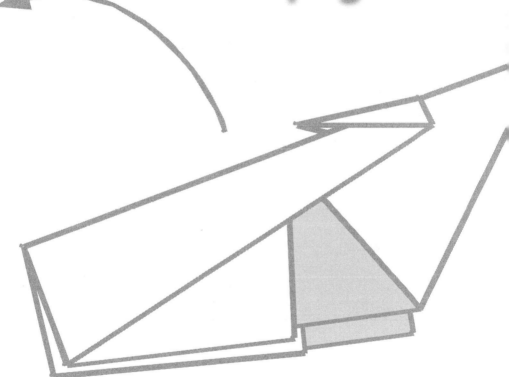

n the low-volatility environment before the dollar was set free in 1971, Wall Street was primarily about relationships, private partnerships transferring risk as agents. It was a club, a guild. The jump in volatility after severing the link between gold and the dollar and after interest rates were set loose a decade later boosted the need for risk management tools and helped give rise to the dominance of the traders over bankers. This, in turn, gave rise to Wall Street firms becoming *public companies* using other people's money as *principals* of risk transfer as opposed to *partnerships* and *agents* transferring it. The return to a low-volatility environment after 2002 left little risk to *transfer* or *assume,* so Wall Street began to *manufacture* it, much the way companies manufacture synthetic rubber, oil, and diamonds.

Since 1981, the "agent-driven" and the "principal-driven" departments in Wall Street firms have competed against each other for who generated the most revenue and profits. Recall the way Phibro and Salomon turned the tables on each other in 1981, when oil prices were high and bond prices low, and in 1986, when oil prices crashed and bond prices soared, bond traders and bankers swapped places in terms of revenue and profit contribution, as well as who controlled the firm. Whatever market was doing "better" seemed to get the upper hand. For example, bond traders were ascendant in the ranks of Wall Street management in the early 1990s. Of the top five investment banks, four were run by former traders. The 1993–1994 bear market in bonds, the worst in six decades, dealt them a setback. That bear market helped the bankers regain influence and drive revenue during the dot-com boom of 1995–1999, when they relaxed the standards for initial public offerings, no longer requiring them to have three years' profitability before going public. This effectively refolded the IPO process and ran a good idea into the ground.

Cracks in the Wall Street business model had formed by 2001 when the corporate scandals and record-setting bankruptcies called into question analyst recommendations (conflicts of interest in getting investment banking business), auditor opinions (conflicts of interest in auditing companies and providing tax advice), and accounting practices (off-balance sheet SPEs to hide debt).

By 2002, the bankers had sullied their names, having breached the Chinese Wall that was supposed to separate them from sales and research and having been sued by New York Attorney General Eliot Spitzer for doing so. Coupled with a stock market cut in half in two years, there was little investment banking business. The crashing stock market and a booming mortgage market put bond traders back in control.

Deal makers' influence declined, and the traders again rose. At Goldman Sachs Group Inc., from 2000–2002, revenue from the fixed-income trading unit (which also includes currencies and commodities at the firm) grew 49 percent to a record $4.47 billion. At Morgan Stanley, the fixed income trading division in 2002 generated $3.27 billion of revenue, or *more than three times* the $962 million that it made from advising companies on acquisitions. In 2002, Bear Stearns had its most profitable year since going public in 1984. The firm got 41 percent of its revenue from its fixed-income trading division, more than any rival that year. The division generated record revenue of $1.9 billion, *more than double* that of its investment banking unit.[1] The bull market in stocks beginning in October 2002 coincided with several marker events that would drive Wall Street revenue and profits for the next five years. The nascent credit derivatives market had been "tested" by the biggest bankruptcies in U.S. history, as well as the largest sovereign default in history, Argentina, and survived. WorldCom Inc's $104 billion bankruptcy filing in July 2002 shattered the previous record, filed by Enron seven months previously, and held the embarrassing label of the biggest bankruptcy, until the Lehman Brothers' $639 billion filing in 2008. Lehman was one-and-one-half times larger than the next nine largest bankruptcies in U.S. history. It was more than three times the size of WorldCom and Enron combined, as shown in Table 7.1.

"Up until 2002, we hadn't been tested as a market; now we know," said Andrew Palmer, who marketed credit derivatives at J.P. Morgan Chase. "In each of these occurrences, the product came through with flying colors."[2]

As if on cue, in September 2002 Fed Chairman Greenspan praised credit derivatives in a London speech: "These increasingly complex financial instruments have been special contributors, particularly over the past

Table 7.1 The Ten Largest U.S. Bankruptcy Filings

Company	Assets ($ billions)	Date Filed
Lehman Brothers Holdings Inc.	639.0	09/15/2008
WorldCom Inc.	103.9	07/21/2002
Enron Corp.	63.4	12/02/2001
Conseco Inc.	61.4	12/18/2002
Texaco Inc.	35.9	04/12/1987
Financial Corp. of America	33.9	09/09/1988
Refco Inc.	33.3	10/17/2005
IndyMac Bancorp Inc.	32.7	07/31/2008
Global Crossing Ltd.	30.2	01/28/2002
Calpine Corp	27.2	12/20/2005

DATA SOURCE: Bloomberg Financial, L.P.

couple of stressful years, to the development of a far more flexible, efficient and resilient financial system than existed just a quarter century ago."[3]

Low Volatility, Low Risk

"The Great Moderation," a phrase coined to describe the decline in volatility in the economy and financial markets, first appeared in the press the same month.[4] Lower volatility meant less risk, the very product in which Wall Street trafficked. Credit derivatives had helped investors and traders *manage risk* more effectively. *Spreading risk* through the financial system *reduced volatility.* In October, the Fed cut its benchmark overnight interest rate to 1.75 percent, lower than inflation as measured by the Consumer Price Index (CPI) and thus creating *negative real interest rates.* The bull market in stocks started the same month, and the Fed maintained a negative interest rate environment for three and a half years, the longest period of time since 1971. By the end of 2002, Wall Street settled the Spitzer and SEC investigations, and the EU imposed a rule that would influence how U.S. Wall Street firms financed themselves (more on that rule below).

Traders thrive on volatility because price swings afford opportunities to profit and to exact wider bid-ask spreads when making markets for others. It was the *very volatility* unleashed on financial markets in 1971 when the dollar unhinged from gold and when interest rate ceilings ended a decade later *that provided* the incentives for Wall Street's risk-transfer transactions to migrate from agent-driven to principal-driven businesses.

The risk environment became so subdued that from the start of the bull market on October 9, 2002, through February 26, 2007, the S&P 500 Index had neither a 10 percent decline, nor a single-day drop of more than 2 percent. Corporate borrowers, who cannot guarantee interest and principal payments, could borrow for as little as 49 basis points (or half a percent) more than the rate paid by the U.S. Treasury, which guaranteed repayment. Figure 7.1 shows the general decline in volatility in stock prices as measured by the Standard & Poor's 100 implied volatility

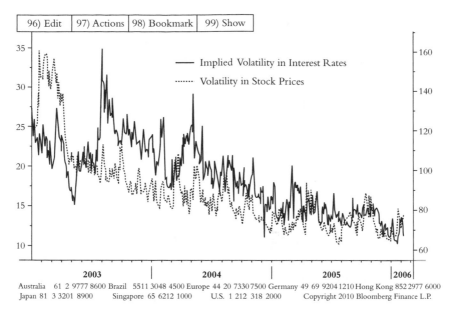

| 96) Edit | 97) Actions | 98) Bookmark | 99) Show |

—— Implied Volatility in Interest Rates
········ Volatility in Stock Prices

Australia 61 2 9777 8600 Brazil 5511 3048 4500 Europe 44 20 7330 7500 Germany 49 69 9204 1210 Hong Kong 852 2977 6000
Japan 81 3 3201 8900　　Singapore 65 6212 1000　　U.S. 1 212 318 2000　　Copyright 2010 Bloomberg Finance L.P.

Figure 7.1　Volatility in Stocks and Interest Rates Declined after 2002 (annual percent)
Source: Bloomberg Financial, L.P.

index. It gauges how volatile investors think prices will be over the coming month. The figure also shows the decline in interest rate volatility, as measured by a Merrill Lynch's index gauging options prices.

Low volatility meant little risk, little to transfer as an agent, and little to assume as a principal. When the price of an industry's product declines, in order to maintain profit levels, much less increase them, it must:

1. Produce more of it
2. Introduce "new-and-improved" versions with a higher price, and/or
3. Borrow money to leverage returns

Wall Street did all three.

In 2002, the low-volatility environment that previously prevailed in the "agent era" descended upon an industry then run by traders willing to assume risk that was in scarce supply just as *Great Moderation* became part of the lexicon. Bankers were out of fashion and traders were in.

The previous such low-risk environment was pre-1971, when Wall Street was primarily about relationships: private partnerships transferring risk as agents. The jump in volatility after the dollar was set free from gold in 1971 and interest rates were set loose a decade later helped give rise to Wall Street firms as public companies using other people's money as *principals* of risk transfer. The low volatility environment after 2002 left little risk to *transfer* or *assume,* so Wall Street began to *manufacture* it, much the way companies manufacture synthetic rubber, or synthetic oil, and even synthetic diamonds.

The CDS Market Develops

The CDS market developed much the way the interest rate swaps market did after the IBM-World Bank deal in 1981: Bankers looked at client lists to identify ones who might benefit from similar swaps, arranging the deals as an agent again, transferring risk between parties from those afraid interest might rise and those afraid they would fall. Next, the banks became market makers (principals) in interest rate swaps for clients and other banks. Finally, interest rate swaps became a favored speculative vehicle for betting on changes in interest rates. When the hedge fund Long-Term Capital Management blew up in September 1998, it had 10,000 swap positions speculating on historical price relationships.

Similarly, in the CDS market, the banks initially used them to shift risk and avoid regulatory capital requirements; institutional investors took the other side of the trade from the banks to gain exposure to a market previously closed to them by selling CDSs. They collected a bigger income stream than what was available from bank accounts or U.S. Treasury securities. Next, commercial banks, investment banks, and insurance companies became market makers for customers and other market makers alike. Finally, they began to use CDSs to make proprietary speculative bets on the creditworthiness of corporate and government bonds. Figure 7.2 shows the market grew to $62 trillion in 2007 from $800 billion in 2002.

Pull Neck Upright

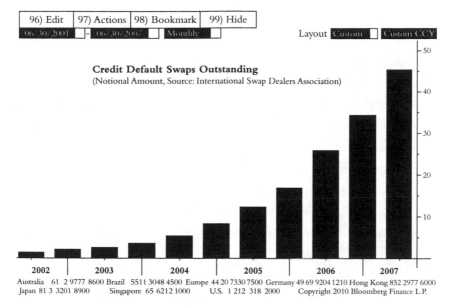

| 96) Edit | 97) Actions | 98) Bookmark | 99) Hide |

Figure 7.2 Credit Default Swaps Outstanding (notional amount, trillions of U.S. $)
SOURCE: Bloomberg Financial, L.P., International Swap Dealers Association.

Thus, as financial markets became more volatile after the dollar and interest rates were set free to float or sink, the firms initially, passively, as a service to clients, assumed the risk as market makers. Eventually, the firms began to initiate positions in the market by trading the firm's capital as "proprietary" traders who might also trade against the positions of clients. In the volatile environment, selectively assuming risk offered opportunities to profit.

In this speculative capacity, a CDS *does not transfer* or *shift* the risk *inherent* in a loan or bond. An investor, generally an institutional investor, can also gain exposure to the risk and higher interest rates of a single corporate name, an index of companies, or a sovereign government. And a CDS can also be used as side bet on whether the reference name—a company, sovereign government, or some index of reference names— will be downgraded or have some other sort of credit-event breaching the terms of the indenture. In this type of transaction, the party seeking "protection" does not have, and likely has no intention of having, direct access to the interest available on bank loans, mortgages, corporate bonds, or sovereign bonds in question. That is, these CDSs *manufactured synthetic exposure* to the risks accompanying these reference securities. The transactions have nothing to do with protecting against the risk inherent (i.e., that of a credit event) in owning a bond or loan. Lacking an economic interest and risk of loss in debt of the reference company, they were speculative transactions.

As we've seen, Wall Street's business is to transfer risk, the kind ever-present in a free market economy. Management guru Peter Drucker calls it "risk which is coincident with the commitment of present resources to future expectations."[5] It can also be called *inherent risk,* part of the everyday markets in which we participate as consumers, such as the department store, grocery store, and gas station. The producers bear the financial risks associated with getting the product to the consumer. This type of risk is often managed via derivatives on the centralized exchanges and over-the-counter financial markets.

Manufactured risk, on the other hand, creates a potential monetary loss that otherwise would not have existed had not the bet been made. The risk is not a by-product of an activity itself. The roulette wheel could be spun, the football game played, and the horse race run without monetary loss occurring. Wagering on the outcome of any of these events creates risk.

The gambling game roulette offers an analogy to explain the created risk that built up in the financial system during the low-volatility environment of 2002–2007. Betting on red 36 and doubling down every time it loses will eventually have a huge payoff, if the bettor's money can last long enough. Betting *against* red 36 and doubling up every time it paid off, which was often, generates steadily increased income but will eventually generate a huge loss. *This was akin to traders providing loss protection via credit default swaps, "selling" them to collect the premium.* So long as no "credit events" occurred, the provider kept the premium and did not have to pay anything out.

More Insurance Than Needed

Credit default swaps *are not* insurance contracts, technically speaking; they *are not* regulated as insurance contracts. Insurance is a contract for compensation to protect against loss; one doesn't have to be exposed to any loss in order to enter CDSs. They do not require the buyer to have an economic interest in the underlying asset—which is not so much a problem in derivatives where the underlying is an asset. They are effectively a series of option contracts folded together via Financial Origami. This gives the CDS seller a series of premium payments rather than just one, as is the case with an option. The CDSs *can* perform the function of insurance; but they *can also* perform one of speculation.

Consider the following scenario: Your house burns down. Fortunately, you have fire insurance, so you call the insurance company to report the loss and file a claim. The next day, your agent meets you in front of the property, and the agent writes you a check. Suddenly, several neighbors arrive with hands extended, asking the agent for their check because they too had taken out a fire insurance policy on your home. They had no risk of loss in your home; in fact, no economic interest in it at all until they took out the insurance policies, and then only an interest in seeing it burn to the ground.

They may have taken out a policy, but it was not with the agent cutting the check to you. (And no mention is made just yet of what involvement any of the neighbors may have had in setting the property ablaze in the first place.) The neighbors must collect from whoever sold them the policies on a house that was not their own. In this example, risk was created. You had an inherent risk, because it was your property. The neighbors' insurance policies created, or manufactured, potential risk because it was *not* their property. They had no insurable interest in the house.

What would have prompted the neighbors to take out the policies? They might have noticed that you often cooked on an open grill on the wooden deck attached to your house, drank a lot, and often passed out while the fire raged on the grill. They may just have sensed a potential opportunity. Alternatively, they may not have liked you and intended to burn your house, picking up a few dollars in the process.

Take the example a step further. Say that 20 neighbors had each taken out a fire insurance policy on your house, each making annual premium payments to a single "insurance" company. Now envision that company creates a $10 million financial instrument, the coupon of which is the 20 neighbors' annual premiums, and that some institutional investor buys the security. Now think about it. Their "investment" has no underlying asset; rather it has the opposite, a liability. When the house burns down, the $10 million goes to pay the 20 neighbors' insurance policies. And the investor gets what? The land and pile of smoldering rubble? No. And certainly there's no way to get it 20 times over, once for each neighbor.

Consider an alternative scenario. You sell fire insurance policies on each of the homes in a subdivision, package the premiums and offer that as a cash flow to, say, a pension fund. All of the monthly premiums (cash flows) are passed through to the fund, except for a small servicing charge, which you keep. If one of the homes burns down, the pension fund suffers a relatively small loss, having to pay out the insurance claim to you. If fire sweeps through the neighborhood and all the homes burn down, the pension suffers a complete loss because it is liable to pay your insurance claims on all of the homes.

In sum, you can't have more insurance outstanding than there are insurable assets, unless you are on Wall Street. Theoretically, it's logical that a given asset might have an equal quantity of derivatives outstanding; the contracts allow asset owners the ability to hedge the inherent risk of holding the asset if they so choose. For liquidity's sake, it even makes sense for there to be more derivatives than underlying assets. It might make sense for the market to create $2 billion is CDSs on a company with $1 billion in debt outstanding. But it is also true that the extra billion is not "necessary." As just one example, when Delphi, the auto parts maker, went bankrupt in 2005, the CDSs on its debt exceeded the value of its bonds tenfold.[6]

The speculative element in a market (i.e., at least one party to a transaction has no vested business-risk interest) helps provide market liquidity, the ability to buy or sell quickly without causing big changes in price. The same phenomenon occurs in other derivatives markets, such as futures contracts listed on commodity exchanges, helping to fill the function of price discovery. For example, the New York Mercantile Exchange's daily volume in crude oil futures in 2009 averaged about 550 million barrels a day. That's about *six times* the daily global consumption of oil.

Companies with exposure to oil prices, as well as speculators with no such exposure, are trading in that market. The exchange has standardized contracts with trade reporting, price transparency, and daily posting of capital as surety margin to demonstrate participants' ability and willingness to honor the contracts. Exchanges provide price and volume transparency in real time. An exchange's clearinghouse is the counterparty in all futures and options contracts and promises to make good on all transactions. To make sure prices are not being manipulated, speculators holding more than a specified number of exchange-traded contracts are required to report those positions to the Commodity Futures Trading Commission at least weekly. Leading up to the crisis, there was no such reporting requirement, however, for OTC swaps, which the President's Working Group recommended be exempt from regulation in November 1999, the same month Glass-Steagall was repealed.

Opaque Markets

While OTC markets enable more-tailored products, by their very nature they are less liquid than standardized contracts on exchanges. Importantly, certain accounting rules for hedging require matching maturities of hedges to exposure, which means companies have a strong incentive to use the OTC market, which can tailor such dates. These OTC products offer opportunities for large profits because transaction prices are not posted for all to see and compare.

As with most things on Wall Street, this is nothing new. Historian Fernand Braudel notes the rise in the fortunes of those engaged in *"private trading"* (emphasis his). With the increased population and economic growth of sixteenth-and seventeenth-century England, the existing network of regular markets became inadequate. "The initiators of such private trading were 'substantial' traveling merchants, pedlars and salesmen: they went around to the kitchen doors of farms to buy up in advance wheat, barley, sheep, wool, poultry, rabbit-skins, and sheepskins." Private trading "was simply a way of getting round the open or public market which was closely supervised," writes Braudel.[7]

In the long-dated OTC contracts, five-year CDSs, for example, there was often no daily posting of margin to maintain a good faith deposit between the counterparties the way there *is* on exchange-traded derivatives. This allowed losses in some positions to accumulate over a much longer time than the typical one-month to three-month tenor of exchange-traded contracts. For example, a futures contract expiring on a three-month cycle requires daily posting of good faith margin *and* a whole new contract and recommitment of the higher initial margin to re-establish the position every three months. In privately negotiated OTC contracts, that is not always the case.

Moreover, the risk profile of CDSs differs from exchange-traded derivatives. The trigger event compelling fulfillment of the CDS contract terms is so severe for the underlying credit that the price of the CDS can surge by enormous amounts when the event threatens. The potential, or latent, volatility in credit-default swaps compared to futures contracts was underscored by the Lehman Brothers bankruptcy in September 2008. Figure 7.3 shows that over a three-day period, the annual cost to insure $10 million of debt for Morgan Stanley jumped from $262,000 to $998,000.

The volatility, or risk, covering a 10-day period soared above 500 percent. That was more than three times as great as the highest 10-day volatility for crude oil when the price fell from a record of more than $147 a barrel to about $45 in the second half of 2008. The volatility gauge

Pull Neck Upright

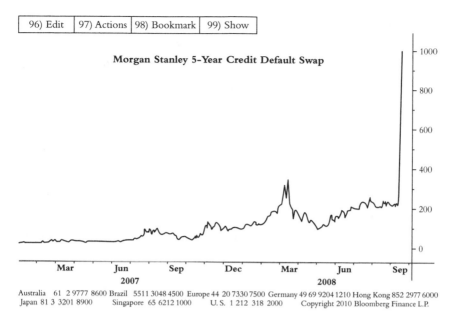

Morgan Stanley 5-Year Credit Default Swap

Australia   61 2 9777 8600 Brazil 5511 3048 4500 Europe 44 20 7330 7500 Germany 49 69 9204 1210 Hong Kong 852 2977 6000
Japan 81 3 3201 8900   Singapore 65 6212 1000   U. S. 1 212 318 2000   Copyright 2010 Bloomberg Finance L.P.

Figure 7.3   Morgan Stanley Five-Year CDS March to September 2008 (basis points)
SOURCE: Bloomberg Financial, L.P.

compares closing prices over a 10-day period and annualizes how much they differ from the average, in annual percentage terms. This "jump-to-default" payout feature makes it difficult to manage the risks of CDSs.[8]

The party entering the sell-side of a CDS assumes a potential, or contingent, liability the same way the companies selling fire insurance on your house did in the example above. If the party taking out the protection at least has underlying bonds (a so-called funded CDS), impaired though they may be, there are bonds to hand over much the way a car owner would turn over the totaled car in exchange for the blue book value payment from the insurance company. The car can be sold for parts or to a junkyard. In a so-called unfunded CDS, there is nothing to turn over; it is purely a side bet.

And a synthetic CDO made up of the payments on CDSs also has no asset underlying it. Rather, the CDO securitizes the cash flow of "premiums" received in exchange for providing "make whole" insurance in case a bond, loan, or mortgage has a credit event, such as a downgrade to below investment grade or a default. So the low volatility environment led to manufacturing risk by selling CDSs for the income.

Securitizing income streams from corporate assets takes the form of stocks and bonds; securitizing the stream from mortgages form mortgage-backed securities (MBS); securitizing income streams from credit card receivables made for asset-backed-securities (ABS). In an ultimate act of Financial Origami, the synthetic CDO effectively *securitizes a liability*. Instead of being used as a derivative *on* a reference asset or entity, the CDS premium payments were *in* the CDO. (More on this in Chapter 8.)

Other People's Money: Debt

As the traditional business lines became more efficient and the margins dropped, many Wall Street firms decided that high-powered commercial banking earning interest rate spreads with borrowed money was an easy fix. Technology and competition had eroded profit margins from commissions, and a bear market in stocks had done the same to underwriting, so the big five investment banks boosted their leverage ratios especially after the Federal Reserve pushed its target rate to a record low 1.5 percent in 2002.

Low volatility meant little risk, little to *transfer* as an agent, and little to *assume* as a principal. Recall the avenues open to firms in an industry in which prices for its product are falling: offer a new and improved version, manufacture and sell more of the product, and/or borrow money. To maintain or boost profits, Wall Street did all three:

1. Offered "new and improved products" (CDSs on individual names and indexes)
2. Manufactured risk (synthetic CDOs; packaged CDS premiums as income streams)
3. Borrowed money to leverage returns

Pull Neck Upright

When Congress replaced Glass-Steagall with Gramm-Leach-Bliley in 1999, it created Investment Bank Holding companies, a new type of entity. It also left a regulator gap, an inconsistency for computing capital adequacy at the holding company, or parent, level versus at the broker-dealer level, where securities are bought and sold. This was an issue of how much *dead capital* securities and brokerage firms should have to set aside as a buffer against loss for particular financial instruments, including credit derivatives.

As *Great Moderation* entered the lexicon in 2002, as credit derivatives earned praise for blunting the effects of record bankruptcies, and as the stock market bottomed, the European Parliament and the Council of the European Union issued a directive on how credit institutions, insurance, and investment firms would be regulated in Europe. Under the directive, financial market regulators in the European Union would determine if a company of non–EU parentage would be supervised by the EU unless the parent back in the country of origin was supervised on an "equivalent" basis as financial market regulators in Europe.

This was akin to telling Americans that their soldiers in Iraq would be under the command of the generals from another country, France, for instance. Needless to say, the plan did not go over well with the U.S. firms. So Wall Street firms lobbied the SEC, which voted to exempt the Wall Street "bulge bracket" firms from net capital rules. This allowed the five largest firms brokerages to keep less cash on hand and less dead capital provided they file financial reports with the SEC and submit to inspections. Broker-dealers, which are any firms paid commissions in the purchase or sale of securities, are required to keep a specified amount of cash on hand to protect investors should their parent company fail. The new rule allowed the firms to calculate capital reserve requirements using a risk-based formula that included unsecured assets. It also allowed the firms to pile on more debt.

Wall Street had already used other people's money in the equity markets by going public (ownership); now the Street was going after other people's money by borrowing it (loanership). Goldman's leverage ratio, measuring assets relative to equity, was 26.2 times at the end of fiscal year 2007 up from 17.1 times at the end of the 2001 recession. Morgan Stanley's jumped to 32.6 from 23.6, Merrill Lynch's to 31.94 from 19.37, and Lehman's 30.75 from 27.03.

Banks could make easy money holding U.S. Treasury securities instead of lending, and Treasuries required no capital set-aside. Think how much more the Wall Street firms could make owning CDOs that had much higher interest rate than Treasuries and for which they had to set aside less regulatory capital than holding the loans themselves. Loans on a bank's books might require regulatory set-aside capital of about 4 percent. Once securitized and tranched, the same loans required only about a 3 percent capital set-aside. Thus, the incentive for banks to repackage sub-prime mortgages into AAA-rated bonds and invest in them. It was a clever bit of Financial Origami. Wall Street firms effectively became of their own best customers. For example, Fannie Mae and Freddie Mac borrowed from the public at government-subsidized low interest rates and invested that money in the mortgage-backed securities it was creating as part of its mandate. Similarly, bankers, instead of just securitizing mortgages via CDOs, went the extra step and began to borrow in the overnight market to invest the CDOs they were creating.

From 2002 to 2007 Goldman's balance sheet grew to more than $1 trillion from $356 billion, Morgan Stanley's to more than $1 trillion from $529 billion, Merrill Lynch's to $1 trillion from $448 billion, and Lehman Brothers' to $700 billion from $260 billion. Over the same period, investment banks became commercial banks, lending money without credit insight or a deposit base, and commercial banks became brokers, selling securities without market insight.

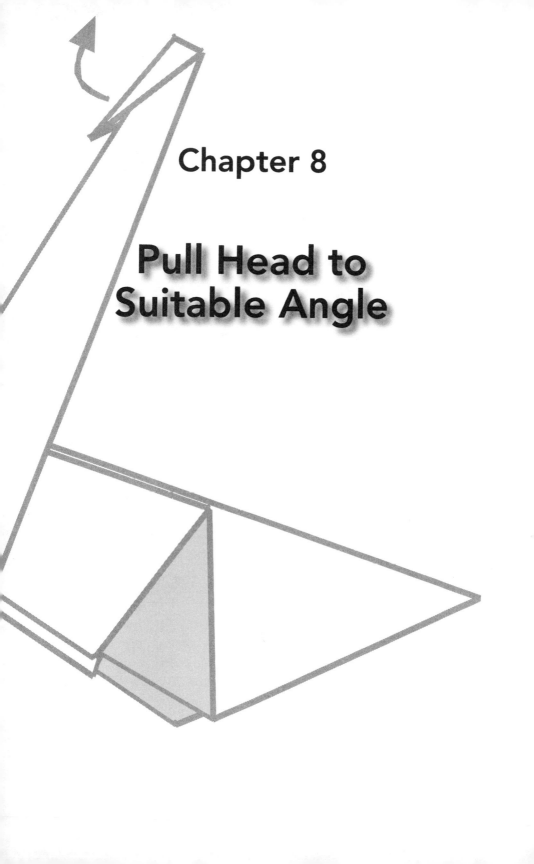

Chapter 8

Pull Head to Suitable Angle

T he simplicity of Wall Street's business model has long been masked by the apparent complexity of its innovations, what some call "financial engineering" and what I call Financial Origami. It's an apt metaphor to capture how the attributes of a few basic products can be folded into new products and the fact that finance is an art, not a science.

Wall Street's job is to transfer risk from those who don't want it to those who do, using one or more of its core three pieces of paper: stock, bond, and derivative. Stocks and corporate bonds transfer risk from the company to those who want to take a chance on its future earnings by securitizing them. Sovereign and municipal debt securitizes expected tax receipts and transfers the risk that they will fall short of expenditures. Derivatives offer an insurance-like protection from financial losses, transferring risk to a third party. The variations on these products aren't as complex as they sound or look. The firms simply fold and refold the three pieces of paper into intricate designs, with new names and higher prices.

The derivatives that people are perplexed by are variations on pieces of paper that have been around for a very long time: futures are as old as medieval fairs; options are recorded in Aristotle's *Politics*; swaps dated from when people lived in caves. Derivatives are an insurance-like contract binding participants to perform transactions in the future if a specified event happens. Figure 8.1 shows the timeline of reintroduction of these

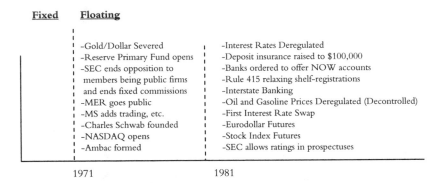

Fixed   Floating

-Gold/Dollar Severed   -Interest Rates Deregulated
-Reserve Primary Fund opens   -Deposit insurance raised to $100,000
-SEC ends opposition to   -Banks ordered to offer NOW accounts
 members being public firms   -Rule 415 relaxing shelf-registrations
 and ends fixed commissions   -Interstate Banking
-MER goes public   -Oil and Gasoline Prices Deregulated (Decontrolled)
-MS adds trading, etc.   -First Interest Rate Swap
-Charles Schwab founded   -Eurodollar Futures
-NASDAQ opens   -Stock Index Futures
-Ambac formed   -SEC allows ratings in prospectuses

1971   1981

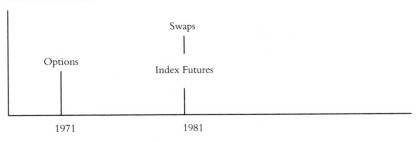

The 3 Derivatives

Options   Swaps   Index Futures

1971   1981

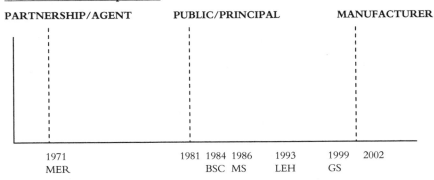

Wall Street Relationship to Risk

PARTNERSHIP/AGENT   PUBLIC/PRINCIPAL   MANUFACTURER

1971   1981 1984 1986   1993   1999   2002
MER   BSC MS   LEH   GS

Figure 8.1 The Inflection Dates for Rules, New Products, and Business Organization

instruments, the major changes in the regulatory environment, and the timeline of the bulge bracket firms going public.

Market participants can do several things with these instruments: invest, trade, speculate, bet, or gamble.[1] But the vehicles themselves are just pieces of paper, some with prettier shapes or more clever designs than others. As we've seen, Wall Street's Financial Origami wasn't limited to the products in which it traffics. In 1971, the bulge bracket firms began refolding their charters into public companies from private partnerships after the New York Stock Exchange dropped a rule prohibiting its members from using that corporate structure.

The trend accelerated after 1981, and Wall Street migrated from being agents of risk transfer to principals of it, more willing to take the other side of the trade in order to facilitate customers' orders. It used other people's money raised in the public offerings to finance the increased trading, but retained the compensation structure, typically 50 percent of revenue.

Wall Street had also begun to refold the industry. Whereas firms once specialized, now they sought to offer one-stop shopping for all financial services. Morgan Stanley, to take but one example, was an investment bank for decades and only added investment management, equities research, and government bond trading in 1971. This vertical structure left the Street vulnerable to conflicts of interest to which it has periodically succumbed over the years, most prominently during the Internet boom when Wall Street bankers and analysts used research to promote stocks of companies in order to get investment banking business from clients.

Wall Street also applied Financial Origami to the mortgage-lending process, unbundling the origination, funding, and servicing components so they could be carried out by separate companies. For decades, banks and savings and loans had performed all three functions and kept the mortgages until they were paid off.

This Financial Origami gave incentives to grant loans bankers previously might never have made. Increasingly, they were low quality and didn't conform to the standards set by government-sponsored enterprises,

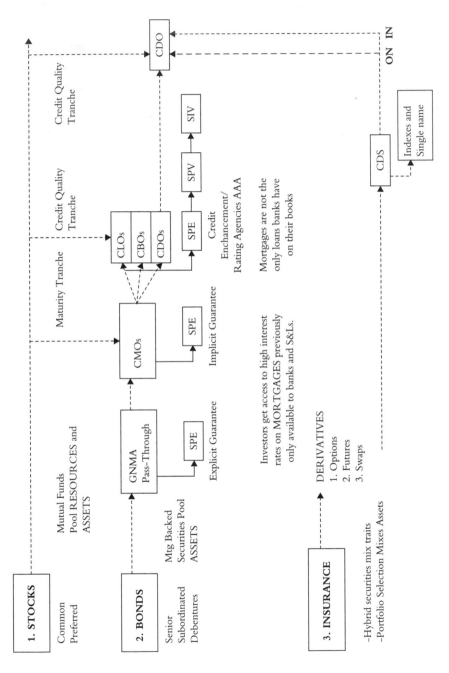

Figure 8.2 Financial Origami Diagram

such as Fannie Mae and Freddie Mac, which also bundled, insured, and sold mortgages as bonds to investors. They even held some of the insured mortgages in their own portfolio and bought ones they'd previously issued. These two government agencies bought and held as much as 40 percent of the total issuance securitized subprime mortgages in 2003 and 2004 as part of the government's effort to increase homeownership.[2]

The risk of the subprime loans wasn't *prepayment*, as it was in the case of government- and agency-backed mortgages, but *nonpayment*. These products passed default losses nonexistent with mortgages from Ginnie Mae, Fannie Mae, and Freddie Mac on to investors as well as passing on interest and principal payments.

The ultimate folding of paper wasn't credit default swaps, and there is nothing wrong with the product per se. The fold that eventually accelerated much of the meltdown in the crisis was CDOs made up of CDS payments or CDSs *inside* of CDOs. That is, bankers packaged CDS premium payments and sold that cash flow as though it came from an asset. It turned out to be one fold too many. Wall Street wasn't securitizing an asset; it was securitizing a potential liability. Anyone buying a synthetic CDO was accepting a contingent liability to have to pay out in case of a credit event. Securitizing cash flows from an income producing asset had become securitizing insurance premiums in exchange for accepting liability. Figure 8.2 shows the completed Financial Origami diagram that we started in Chapter 2.

Vindicating Greenspan

Long before Alan Greenspan's alleged mea culpa during the October 23, 2008, congressional hearing, and long after it as well, his critics blamed him for the U.S. subprime crisis in 2007 that morphed into the global financial crisis in 2008. As the chairman of the Federal Reserve, with a staff of 200 PhDs at his disposal, he should have seen the crisis coming and should have raised interest rates sooner and faster than the Board actually did, say his detractors. They say the Fed's sub-2-percent overnight interest rate in 2002 and 2003 "caused" the housing bubble to form and the Fed's failure to raise rates fast enough and high enough in 2004–2006 allowed the bubble to grow.

Greenspan responded to his critics in a paper titled "The Crisis," published March 9, 2010, the first anniversary of the end of the 17-month bear market in U.S. stocks. In the paper, Greenspan says the Fed *could not have caused* the housing boom, because it was a global property boom, and given that the Fed is not responsible for monetary policy for all those other countries, something else is to blame. He says what *did* cause the bubble was the high and rising savings rates in fast-growing developing countries, coupled with global capital mobility, a topic we touched upon in the Introduction. According to Greenspan, the savings rate of the developing world rose to 34 percent of nominal GDP by 2007 from about 24 percent in 2000. In the same period, real GDP growth in the developing world grew more than double that of the developed. Those savings are what helped finance the *global* property boom of 2002–2007.

In the paper, Greenspan also lays some blame on the U.S. government itself.

> Another factor . . . was the heavy purchases of subprime securities by Fannie Mae and Freddie Mac, the major U.S. Government Sponsored Enterprises (GSE). Pressed by the Department of Housing and Urban Development and the Congress to expand "affordable housing commitments," they chose to meet them by investing heavily in subprime securities. The firms accounted for an estimated 40% of all subprime mortgage securities (almost all adjustable rate), newly purchased and retained on investors' balance sheets during 2003 and 2004.

According to Greenspan, by the first quarter of 2007, when HSBC's write-down announcement touched off the subprime crisis, "virtually all subprime originations were being securitized (compared with only half in

2000), and subprime mortgage securities outstanding totaled more than $900 billion, a rise of more than six-fold since the end of 2001." From 2002 to 2005, subprime mortgages as percent of all mortgages grew to 20 from 7 percent.[3]

There is nothing wrong with subprime mortgages, but the good idea was run into the ground by approving these mortgages on the assumption that rising home prices would enable the borrower to accumulate equity in the house in a few years' time and then use that equity to refinance into a conventional mortgage. That is, expected capital gains in the home price would provide the down payment for a conventional mortgage after two or three years.

How, Not Will, You Pay?

Fair Isaac Corporation (FICO) credit scores became the basis for computerized automated underwriting programs, enabled by the microchip that debuted in 1971. Bankers assigned creditworthiness based on a borrower's past trends in making debt payments. They extrapolated that past repayment behavior into future behavior like most of Wall Street's models did. This failed to take into consideration *how* they would repay. Mortgage originators were basically asking if the borrower *would* repay, not *how*. With a document-light loan, or one in which borrower did not have to provide evidence of income, the "loan officer" was asking "Will you repay on time, based on past behavior?" and not "How will you repay on time?" The loan was granted because both parties thought house prices would rise, and the proceeds from price appreciation would be the equity down payment for a new, conventional mortgage.

FICO scores do not include any gauge of income or employment history, or even the interest rate on its debt outstanding. No cash flow is taken into account. With subprime mortgages, the cash flow presumed is the rising price of the house. Remember, securities are priced as the present value of the cash flows the asset will generate. For stocks this means earnings, and for bonds it's the periodic interest payments and principal repayment of the original loan. In subprime mortgages, the present value presupposed the refinance of the house as part of the cash flows. But that assumed refinancing the house for at least as much as one paid for it, and that assumed house prices never fell.

Greenspan also says the rise in capital flows of global savings in search of higher yields fostered the "global proliferation of securitized, toxic U.S. subprime mortgages," as Greenspan put it, and he notes that the Bank of Canada came to the same conclusion.[4] Figure 8.3 shows global cross-border capital flows rose to 20 percent of global GDP in 2007, up from 5 percent in 2000, according to the McKinsey Global Institute Cross Border Capital Flows database. Figure 8.4 shows the global surge in securitization.

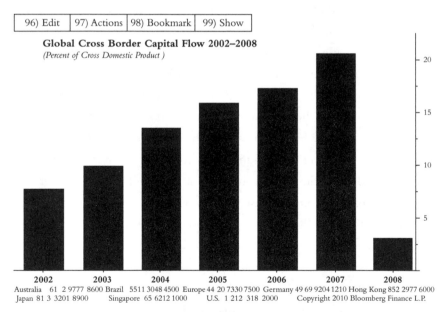

Figure 8.3 Global Cross Border Capital Flows 2002–2008
(percent of GDP)
Source: McKinsey

Pull Head to Suitable Angle

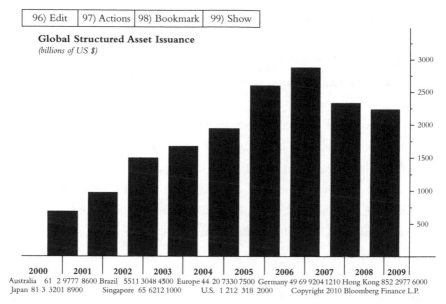

Global Structured Asset Issuance
(billions of US $)

Australia 61 2 9777 8600 Brazil 5511 3048 4500 Europe 44 20 7330 7500 Germany 49 69 9204 1210 Hong Kong 852 2977 6000
Japan 81 3 3201 8900   Singapore 65 6212 1000   U.S. 1 212 318 2000   Copyright 2010 Bloomberg Finance L.P.

Figure 8.4 Global Securitized Asset Issuance 2000–2009

(billions of US $)

SOURCE: McKinsey

Broken Markets

More global savings than investment led to a decline in interest rates around the world, which meant lower monthly mortgage payments. This gave borrowers with spotty credit histories a chance to get a mortgage made more readily available because investors and the GSEs were snapping up bonds backed by pools of subprime mortgages.

Flows into and out of asset classes can distort their prices, pushing them far away from long-term averages or otherwise disconnect from previously established price relationships. In the process, markets can become distorted, even broken. For example, Greenspan had what he called a "conundrum" when the Fed raised its benchmark overnight interest rate starting in June 2004; the yield on the ten-year U.S. Treasury note fell instead of rose. He attributed the phenomenon to a global savings glut wherein foreign investors bought U.S. Treasury securities almost regardless of the yield on the bonds.

Exchange-traded futures contracts, too, have experienced episodes of dysfunctional markets in which the relationship between today's prices and those for future dates broke down. In the spring of 2008, the cotton and wheat markets broke for a similar reason: persistent buying. "The market is broken; it's out of whack," William Dunavant Jr., chairman of cotton merchant Dunavant Enterprises Inc., said on April 22, 2008, at a CFTC conference in Washington examining whether futures markets were working properly.[5] Rising crop futures were pushing small hedgers out of the market and making it difficult for companies to manage risk, he said.

That anomaly arose from another act of Financial Origami. Wall Street bankers offered investors the opportunity to earn returns on commodity futures contracts, especially after the Federal Reserve's sub-2-percent interest rate environment in 2002–2004 (see Figure 8.5). Commodity

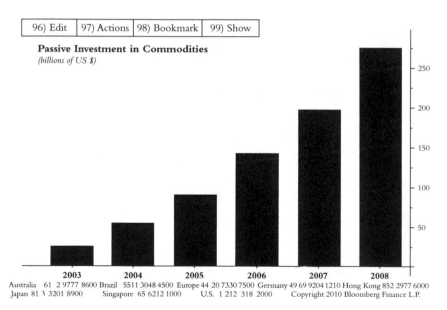

Figure 8.5 Passive Investment in Commodities (billions of US $)
SOURCE: Barclays

Exchange Traded Funds (ETFs) mimicked stock market mutual funds. Investors pooled resources into a fund that used the money to buy commodity futures contracts. When the contracts expired, the fund simply "rolled" into the next month's contract. The funds sold their holdings only when investors in the ETFs wanted out of the asset class. These funds treat commodities as an asset class, and they employed a buy-and-hold strategy in order to gain exposure to price swings in commodities, the way Harry Markowitz's portfolio strategy would have investors do: add uncorrelated assets to a portfolio in order to reduce risk.

By early 2008, futures prices in some commodity markets were well above what users were willing to pay in cash markets. In March that year, the Chicago Board of Trade futures market had contracts for 2.1 billion bushels of wheat on a crop of only 360 million bushels. The cash market and futures market disconnected; the price differentials were much more than could be accounted for by using the typical measures of cost of storage, insurance, and the time value of money. The differential was as much as $2 a bushel compared to a more normal 20 to 40 cents.

The price relationship between the cash and derivative future market was broken. Enabling this phenomenon and aggravating the situation was the fact that the companies offering the ETFs were considered "hedgers" by the regulatory authorities. This meant they had no limit to how much they could buy. Food processors and farmers, whose business dealings, by definition, put them in contact with the commodities, do not have so-called "position limits" that cap the quantity of futures contracts they can hold. Those labeled "speculators" do have limits to prevent manipulation or otherwise distort the market. The firms offering ETFs claimed hedger status because they were selling an "investment" that directly exposed them to the ups and downs of commodity prices. The CFTC permitted it.

A similar disconnect occurred in the subprime mortgage derivatives market, aggravating the financial crisis. Wall Street Financial Origami in January 2006 created an *index on derivatives* instead of directly on a cash market instrument: the ABX.HE, an index of the 20 most liquid CDSs on U.S. subprime mortgages and not the cash price for the underlying mortgages themselves. This enabled a theoretically unlimited number of contracts to be created on the Index *and* CDSs that were not constrained by the size of the cash market both were ultimately referencing. There was no arbitrage to the cash market. The ABX index *created bets on bets.* The Bank for International Settlements reported, "Trade documentation excludes any form of physical settlement, thus decoupling ABX trading from the availability of the underlying cash instruments."[6]

The lack of arbitrage between the index on CDS and the cash market made conditions ripe for "one-way" trades to push the market price to abnormally low levels. It was akin to pushing on a revolving door; there is no countervailing force to keep the move in check, as would be the case in an arbitraged market.

An accounting change further aggravated the financial crisis. The Financial Accounting Standards Board (FASB) imposed an accounting rule that went into effect in November 2007, just as the subprime crisis was spreading to the economy and financial markets. It required companies to use "observable market prices" to value many securities and derivatives, rather than pricing models or cash flows from the instruments. If this so-called mark-to-market showed the securities had declined in price, the company would report that as a loss, reducing net income. Given that the ABX was the only index of subprime mortgages, it became the industry benchmark for valuing securities. It also became the vehicle of choice to get "insurance protection" for any portfolio of subprime mortgages. This added to the "pushing on a revolving door" phenomenon. Traders and investors with CDOs marked down the value of their portfolios as the ABX declined, then some sold the ABX index to protect their positions from further price deterioration. This selling put further downward pressure on the index, forcing another mark down in the mark-to-market process. It was a vicious cycle that did not stop until the mark-to-market rule was modified and made less stringent in March 2009, the exact bottom of the bear market in stocks.

Fair value is supposed to represent the price at which an asset would change hands in an orderly, arm's-length transaction. Advocates of this "fair value," mark-to-market accounting say investors want to see what financial instruments are worth, not just what they cost, and they shouldn't have to dig through the footnotes to find out. Opponents say fair-value marks for illiquid instruments are unreliable, so they shouldn't be mandatory. Their view is that accounting should reflect economic reality, not dictate it.

In any event, one form of mark-to-market *is* responsible for the housing bubble in the first place. Homeowners were marking their houses to market and then using them as automated teller machines to tap equity when prices rose. Without that kind of accounting for homeowners, the bubble likely would not have gotten as big as it did.

In the case of CDSs, some of the firms entering contracts to wager on a company's having financial difficulty may also have extended credit to that same company via the securities repo market. It's one thing for George Bailey to have his depositors withdraw funds and quite another for them to buy CDS on the Building & Loan at the same time. People respond to incentives, and everything else is commentary. Consider a bank with overnight loans to a securities firm. On any given day, the bank can simply refuse to lend to the firm, especially if the collateral is suspect. Or, if the bankers are worried about lending to the company in the overnight repo market because the company may be having financial problems, it's not being malicious to withhold the loan. It makes perfect sense for traders at the bank. This is the equivalent of a run on an investment bank. The typical run on a commercial bank involves running to the bank to make withdrawals. A run on an investment bank is withholding the extension of loans to finance its securities.

Thus, with credit derivatives there is the potential for a destructive cycle that does not occur in futures for agricultural products. This is especially true as related to the potential for a run on the institution, which is what happened with Bear Stearns. The day before the company collapsed into the arms of JPMorgan Chase, Bear Stearns met all regulatory capital requirements. But no one would lend money to Bear overnight because any lender questioned the value of the securities being offered as collateral. The cycle would be akin to accumulating futures contracts on corn, then going out and destroying the fields growing the crops. With credit derivatives, a bank might refuse to lend to a company and then buy CDSs on the troubled firm or vice versa. Six months later, the pattern repeated itself with Lehman; it was starting to happen to Merrill Lynch when Bank of America bought it, as well as Goldman Sachs and Morgan Stanley when they filed to become commercial banks to avoid a "run" on their companies.

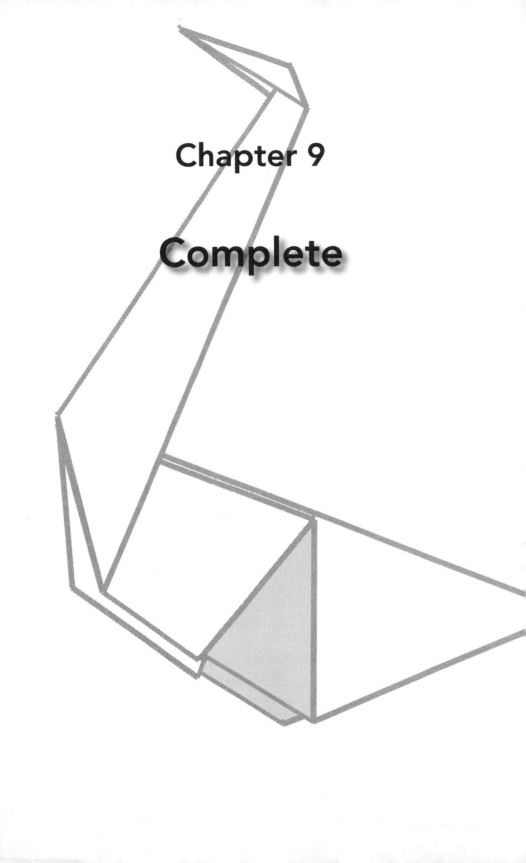

Chapter 9

Complete

I n the Introduction, I invoked the economics axiom that people respond to incentives and everything else is commentary. Airline executives facing government publication of on-time arrival performance, for example, simply lengthened the advertised duration of flights. Similarly, bankers facing regulatory capital rules proved adept at minimizing "dead capital."

Wall Street's job is to transfer risk, whether stocks or bonds or derivatives, and whether in the primary or secondary markets. Risk is a natural product of life in general and the free market economy in particular. Not even the fanciest of academic models can make risk go away. It cannot be removed, only shifted, which Wall Street does via three basic pieces of paper and the Financial Origami it performs on them to form "new" products. And government regulations will not protect you from risk either. Consider that the heart of the financial crisis lay within institutions that may be the most regulated in the United States, behind pharmaceutical companies.

As Merton Miller pointed out, regulation is responsible for most financial innovations, what I call Financial Origami. Worse still, government regulation gives a false sense of security and creates a unique form of moral hazard. This is not an argument for or against more regulation. It's merely to point out that, ultimately, it won't matter and that taxpayers should not delude themselves that their representatives can use new rules to solve problems in the financial markets assuming they understand the problem well enough in the first place.

Some of Senate Banking Committee Chairman Christopher Dodd's remarks when he presented his financial overhaul bill in April 2010 suggest that at least some lawmakers may not even grasp the essence of the crisis. "This legislation will bring transparency and accountability to exotic instruments like hedge funds and derivatives that have for far too long lurked in the shadows of our economy," Dodd said.[1]

Dodd's comment doesn't lend confidence that he even knew what happened. First of all, hedge funds are not instruments. Second, neither the instruments nor hedge funds were catalysts for the financial crisis; regulated financial institutions were. The crisis and subsequent recession shuttered 2,300 hedge funds in 2008 and 2009, according to Chicago-based Hedge Fund Research Inc., and hardly anyone noticed. The only people who suffered were investors in these lightly regulated investment pools, which were not the problem. Rather, the regulated entities were the problem. Worse still, the Act did not address what to do with Fannie Mae and Freddie Mac, which played such an important role in the crisis.

The financial instrument itself is rarely, if ever, the problem. Instead, it's who's using the instrument and for what purpose. A gun in the hands of a police officer is a good thing, but not in the hands of a cop using it to rob people. After all, the Federal Reserve used currency swaps with European central banks to ease money-market conditions when credit markets froze in 2008. And government regulations are to blame for currency swaps in the first place. Capital controls in place from World War II through 1981 forced companies into so-called back-to-back loans, reciprocal agreements to lend money to each other's domestic subsidiaries, and the invention of currency swaps that year circumvented that obstacle.

Remember, derivatives are simply contracts to perform financial transactions in the future. Without them, companies wouldn't be able to hedge the risk of prices changing in the future. Granted, people can speculate with derivatives, but that is true with purchases and sales of stocks and bonds as well.

Accounting tools, too, can be used for a variety of purposes. The terms "off-balance sheet" and "special-purpose entity" came into the popular lexicon when Enron went bankrupt in 2001. Ever since, they've had negative connotations. Yet SPEs make possible some of the safest investments in the world: GNMAs, which are backed by the full faith and credit of the U.S. government.

When announcing his draft bill of what would become the Dodd-Frank Act, Christopher Dodd also said, "This legislation will not stop the next crisis from coming. No legislation can, of course."[2] Maybe that should be the preamble to every set of laws and regulations dealing with financial markets. There is a way around any set of rules, as shown by pyramid-schemer Bernie Madoff, who scammed investors out of $65 billion. His firm was regulated by the SEC, which audited his firm several times. At least with a disclaimer, the police wouldn't be giving citizens a false sense of security.

History suggests that regulators are fighting a losing battle. Regulations create incentives for people to circumvent the very rules being imposed and simultaneously give investors a false sense of security, the government's own special form of moral hazard. The public believes it must be safe if the government has sanctioned the product, entity, or activity. For example, the Sarbanes-Oxley Act of 2002, passed after the series of accounting fraud scandals including Enron Corp. and WorldCom Inc., was hailed as a great investor-protection achievement. Among other things, the Act required officers of the company to attest to the accuracy of financial statements. It failed, though, to prevent accounting gimmicks that contributed to the largest bankruptcy in U.S. history six years later: Lehman Brothers, at $639 billion, was more than triple the Enron and WorldCom filings combined.

Remember also that the SEC provides an aura of validation for ratings companies by allowing financial firms to use the rating opinions for regulatory purposes—that is, for calculating regulatory capital. When Moody's and Standard & Poor's assigned AAA ratings to securities created from subprime mortgages, investors took it as the equivalent of an SEC seal of approval.

Moreover, the government-arranged takeover of Bear Stearns Cos. by JPMorgan Chase & Co. in March 2008 created a special kind of the moral hazard that helped set the stage six months later for the collapse of Lehman as well as the $64.8 billion Reserve Primary money-market fund, which held Lehman debt. The SEC's suit against the fund's parent, Reserve Management Corp., cites e-mail from its chief investment officer who wrote that he "believed Lehman would, if necessary, be assisted by the federal government."

History also shows that Wall Street has been adept at getting around the rules and regulations imposed upon corporate behavior and financial instruments. For example, Bill Clinton's administration in 1993 tried to rein in executive pay by limiting to $1 million the tax deductibility of their cash compensation. Corporations simply offered stock options to skirt the restriction. Enron *hid debt and losses* with off-balance sheet transactions. Lehman used them to *hide assets* to make it appear less leveraged, according to Anton Valukas, the examiner for Lehman's bankruptcy. Greece used currency swaps with Goldman Sachs to *hide debt* to gain entry to the European Union.

What's Wrong with Wall Street?

Wall Street's biggest problems arise from the conflicts of interest inherent in the structure that arose over the past four decades, both at the firm level and the industry level. For example, government-sponsored enterprises

Fannie and Freddie are charged with aiding the public policy objectives for increasing homeownership in the United States, although they owe a duty to their shareholders to maximize profits. Credit-rating agencies, also quasi-government companies, are paid for their ratings by the very companies that will benefit from the highest possible rating. Some investment banks and commercial banks have investment banking operations pushing to investor clients securities underwritten for corporate clients. Some have proprietary trading operations, designed to boost company wealth under the same roof as wealth management units designed to boost clients' wealth; this creates the opportunity to take advantage of client orders. Did it ever make sense for the biggest commercial bank in the United States at the time, Citigroup Inc., to get 10 percent of its net income from one commodity trader?[3] Proprietary trading is a zero-sum game; for every dollar of "profit" that one trader makes, another trader has a "loss" of the same amount. With the government standing behind these banks with taxpayer money, it is supporting both the winner and loser in such transactions. Should government-subsidized and -insured commercial banks be allowed to engage in these sorts of principal risk activities? (The Dodd-Frank Act of 2010 included the so-called Volcker rule, which is supposed to prohibit proprietary trading at banks, but it allows up to 12 years in some cases to implement.)

Government-Sponsored Enterprises

President Franklin Delano Roosevelt created Fannie Mae in 1938 to help banks and savings-and-loan associations finance home mortgages as the economy was emerging from the Great Depression. Rather than lend money to homebuyers, it bought mortgages from the mortgage lenders so they could relend funds to another group of home buyers. The rationale was that the Federal National Mortgage Association, as it was then known, would ensure that lenders always had enough money to make new loans, thus helping make mortgages and homes more affordable for Americans.

A lot has changed since then. Fannie Mae went public in 1970 and operates under a congressional charter while seeking to maximize profit for shareholders. Congress also created the Federal Home Loan Mortgage Corporation in 1970. Over the years, the mission for the GSEs changed to include encouraging lending to minorities and low-income borrowers. The 1977 Community Reinvestment Act compelled banks to lend to these groups. The Act has been revised several times since, but the mission remains the same. To aid in the effort, Congress gave the GSEs targets for how much of their purchases were to be composed of mortgages taken out by minorities and below median-income homebuyers. The White House got in on the act too. In October 2002 as *Great Moderation* entered the lexicon, as credit derivatives earned praise for blunting the effects of record bankruptcies, and as the stock market bottomed, President George W. Bush delivered his "we want everyone in America to own a home" speech, reinforcing the government's effort to extend mortgages to people who could not necessarily afford them.[4]

Other government officials were supporters of Fannie and Freddie, as the excerpts below from congressional hearings show. Senate Banking Committee Chairman Christopher Dodd and House Financial Services Committee Chairman Barney Frank drafted the Restoring American Financial Stability Act of 2010, known as the Dodd-Frank Act. They also have spoken up in defense of Fannie and Freddie over the years, even as Alan Greenspan warned against some of the GSEs practices. For example:

House Financial Services Committee hearing, Sept. 10, 2003:

Rep. Barney Frank (D-Massachusetts):	I worry, frankly, that there's a tension here. The more people, in my judgment, exaggerate a threat of safety and soundness, the more people conjure up the possibility of serious financial losses to the Treasury, which I do not see. I think we see entities that are fundamentally sound financially and withstand some of the disaster scenarios . . .

Complete

House Financial Services Committee hearing, Sept. 25, 2003:

Rep. Frank: I do think I do not want the same kind of focus on safety and soundness that we have in OCC [Office of the Comptroller of the Currency] and OTS [Office of Thrift Supervision]. I want to roll the dice a little bit more in this situation towards subsidized housing . . .

Senate Banking Committee, Feb. 24–25, 2004:

Sen. Thomas Carper (D-Delaware.): What is the wrong that we're trying to right here? What is the potential harm that we're trying to avert?

Federal Reserve Chairman Alan Greenspan: Well, I think that that is a very good question, senator.

What we're trying to avert is we have in our financial system right now two very large and growing financial institutions which are very effective and are essentially capable of gaining market shares in a very major market to a large extent as a consequence of what is perceived to be a subsidy that prevents the markets from adjusting appropriately, prevents competition and the normal adjustment processes that we see on a day-by-day basis from functioning in a way that creates stability. . . . And so what we have is a structure here in which a very rapidly growing organization, holding assets and financing them by subsidized debt, is growing in a manner which really does not in and of itself contribute to either home ownership or necessarily liquidity or other aspects of the financial markets . . .

Sen. Richard Shelby (R-Alabama): [T]he federal government has [an] ambiguous relationship with the GSEs. And how do we actually get rid of that ambiguity is a complicated, tricky thing. I don't know how we do it. I mean, you've alluded

	to it a little bit, but how do we define the relationship? It's important, is it not?
Mr. Greenspan:	Yes. Of all the issues that have been discussed today, I think that is the most difficult one. Because you cannot have, in a rational government or a rational society, two fundamentally different views as to what will happen under a certain event. Because it invites crisis, and it invites instability . . .
Sen. Christopher Dodd (D-Connecticut):	I, just briefly will say, Mr. Chairman, obviously, like most of us here, this is one of the great success stories of all time. And we don't want to lose sight of that and [what] has been pointed out by all of our witnesses here, obviously, the 70% of Americans who own their own homes today, in no small measure, due because of the work that's been done here. And that shouldn't be lost in this debate and discussion . . .

Because of the GSEs' special status, investors believed the government would rescue the firms if they ever ran into trouble, even though each prospectus for new Fannie Mae and Freddie Mac debt explicitly says the government has no such obligation. With government backing assumed, Fannie Mae borrowed in the corporate bond markets on better terms than private companies rated AAA. This gave them a large funding advantage over competitors.

At the same time, private mortgage companies were gaining market share by pushing into subprime loans, as shown in Figure 9.1. Non-agency mortgage-backed securities issuance trebled from 2002 to 2007. In response, Fannie and Freddie lowered their standards to take on high-risk mortgages. These two government agencies bought and held as much as 40 percent of the total issuance securitized subprime mortgages in 2003 and 2004.[5]

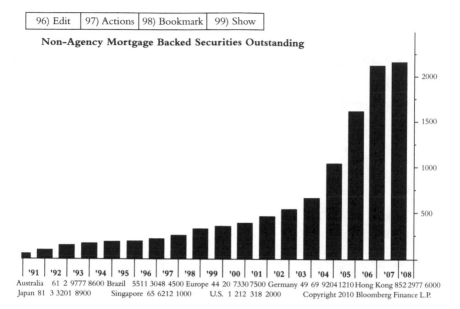

Figure 9.1 Non-Agency MBS Outstanding (billions of U.S. $)
SOURCE: Bloomberg Financial, L.P.

But executives at the GSEs also had shareholders to please as well as an incentive to reach profit goals that determined their bonuses. Because of the implicit U.S. government guarantee, Fannie Mae and Freddie Mac could borrow money for less than their mortgage competitors. They started using their funding advantage to boost profits by increasing purchases of mortgages then holding them as investments rather than selling them as packaged previously issued MBSs. They also bought their own previously packaged MBSs on the open market to hold in their investment portfolios. The profit from these portfolios was greater than what they earned from fees collected in their core business: guaranteeing mortgages to provide liquidity in the secondary market.

Fannie and Freddie owned or guaranteed about 50 percent of the nation's $12 trillion in residential mortgages when the U.S. Treasury Department placed them in conservatorship on September, 7, 2008, giving the American taxpayer an 80 percent ownership interest in the mortgage giants. It also gave them an unlimited bailout pledge from the U.S. government and would become the biggest bailout in U.S. history, reaching $145 billion by the time the New York Stock Exchange delisted the shares on June 16, 2010. The White House's Office of Management and Budget estimated in February 2010 that aid could total as little as $160 billion if the economy strengthens. Private estimates forecast the tab could rise to $1 trillion. Sean Egan, president of Egan-Jones Ratings Co. in Haverford, Pennsylvania, said that a 20 percent loss on the companies' loans and guarantees, along the lines of other large market players such as Countrywide Financial Corp., now owned by Bank of America Corp., could cause even more damage. "One trillion dollars is a reasonable worst-case scenario for the companies," said Egan, whose firm downgraded Enron Corp. a month before its 2001 collapse.[6]

Figure 9.2 shows that Fannie Mae lost more in 2008 alone than it had made cumulatively since going public in 1970. In 2009, the cumulative figure totaled a $72 billion loss. When Fannie and Freddie were placed

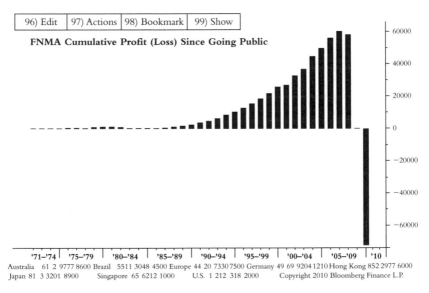

Figure 9.2 FNMA Cumulative Profits/Losses since Going Public (millions of U.S. $)
Source: Bloomberg Financial, L.P.

into conservatorship in September 2008, they had capital of $83 billion supporting about $5.2 trillion of debt and guarantees. That's leveraged 65-to-1, akin to buying a $100,000 house with a $1,493 down payment.

Government-Sanctioned Credit-Rating Agencies

Standard & Poor's and Moody's built their reputations over generations, starting with Henry Varnum Poor's publication in 1860 of "History of Railroads and Canals in the United States" and John Moody's "Moody's Manual of Industrial and Miscellaneous Securities" in 1900. Since the Great Depression, U.S. companies have relied on the agencies to help evaluate the credit quality of investments owned by regulated institutions, gradually bestowing on them quasi-regulatory status. This gave them an aura of government sanction, which would lead to a unique form of moral hazard.

A key feature of the CRAs is their success in defending themselves against litigation by claiming that they are financial information publishers, that their ratings are merely "opinions," and therefore are protected as free speech under the First Amendment.

The SEC's initial regulatory use of the term nationally recognized statistical rating organization (NRSRO) was solely to provide a method for determining capital reserve charges (dead capital) on different grades of debt securities under its net capital rule for broker-dealers. The three biggest rating agencies are Standard & Poor's, Moody's, and Fitch. The main conflict of interest is that they are paid by the companies whose securities they rate. The conflict is akin to those of equity research analysts and investment banking divisions. The analysts held themselves out to be objective in their analysis. However, they were paid by the issuers and bankers, who pressured them to provide bullish recommendations on their worst stocks.

The structured products Wall Street created out of mortgages and other debt were snapped up by investors around the world because of their relatively high interest rates and high credit ratings. Without those

AAA ratings, the gold standard for debt, banks, insurance companies, and pension funds would not have, and in some cases were not permitted to have, bought the products. In order to meet world demand for the AAA-rated, higher-yielding packaged debt, the world's two largest bond-analysis providers repeatedly eased their standards.[7] S&P outlined the process of structured finance in a March 2002 paper for clients entitled "Global Cash Flow and Synthetic CDO Criteria." While arguing that the process "is not alchemy or turning straw into gold," the authors said, "the goal" was to create a capital structure with a higher credit rating than the underlying assets would qualify for individually. The raters estimated the percentage of a debt pool that would pay off, and then assigned AAA grades to the safest portion of the investment and lower marks on the rest. About 85 percent of structured finance CDOs qualified for the top grade, according to Moody's.

Driven by competition for fees and market share, the New York-based companies assigned top ratings on CDOs that included $3.2 trillion of loans to homebuyers with bad credit and undocumented incomes between 2002 and 2007. S&P and Moody's earned as much as three times more for grading CDOs as they did from corporate bonds. Moody's prospectuses don't disclose fees, but it says it charged as much as 11 basis points for structured products, compared with 4.25 basis points for corporate debt. S&P says its fees were comparable.[8] Moody's net income rose to $754 million in 2006, before the subprime crisis struck, from $158 million in 2000, the year it went public. By 2006, structured finance was the companies' leading source of revenue, their financial reports show. It accounted for just under half of Moody's total ratings revenue in 2007. The reckoning swept Wall Street in July 2007, when Moody's cut its grades on $5.2 billion in subprime-backed CDOs. That same day, S&P said it was considering reductions on $12 billion of residential mortgage-backed securities. But this didn't stop them from issuing AAA ratings. Moody's announced AAA grades on at least $12.7 billion of new CDOs in the last week of August 2007. Within three months, five of the investments were lowered by one or both companies within three months and the rest were cut within six months. As subprime borrowers defaulted, the raters downgraded more than three-quarters of the CDOs issued in 2007–2008.

By August 2008, Moody's had downgraded 90 percent of all asset-backed CDO investments issued in 2006 and 2007, including 85 percent of the debt originally rated AAA. S&P had reduced 84 percent of the CDO tranches it rated, including 76 percent of all AAAs. The SEC in July 2008 said S&P and Moody's violated internal procedures and improperly managed the conflicts of interest inherent in providing credit ratings to the banks that paid them.[9]

It's ironic that the quasi-government Fannie, Freddie, and credit rating agencies succumbed to conflicts of interest that fueled the housing bubble and aggravated the bust, yet the government claims it will prevent it from happening again. The government sanctioned and regulated companies played a large role in creating the crisis in the first place.

Banks

Goldman Sachs became the poster child for public anger with Wall Street during the financial crisis when it paid bonuses to its employees after receiving as much as $50 billion in bailout assistance.[10] While Goldman paid out $10.934 billion in compensation in 2008, an average of about $363,546 per employee, 3.623 million Americans lost their jobs. U.S. stock market capitalization collapsed by $7.6 trillion, slashing Americans' savings, and fell $20.3 trillion worldwide.

Five days after Lehman Brothers filed for bankruptcy, Goldman Sachs filed with the Federal Reserve to convert from an investment bank into a commercial bank. Morgan Stanley, the last of the five "bulge bracket" investment banks, did the same. The Fed approved the requests. This gave Goldman Sachs and Morgan Stanley permanent access to the Fed's lending programs, essential to stymie a run on the companies, and probably saved the firms from the fate of Bear Stearns and Merrill Lynch, or worse, Lehman Brothers.

The public and Congress wanted a face of the crisis to blame for all that went wrong. In March 2008, Congress summoned Countrywide Financial

Corp. Chief Executive Officer Angelo Mozilo and former chief executives Charles Prince of Citigroup Inc. and Stan O'Neal of Merrill Lynch & Co. to Capitol Hill to explain their pay packages. Perhaps lawmakers were hoping to find a smoking gun. The witnesses were unfazed, because they had done nothing illegal. Bear Stearns collapsed the following week, and three months later two of its hedge fund managers, Ralph Cioffi and Matthew Tannin, were arrested and accused of misleading investors, who lost $1.6 billion on mortgage investments. They were acquitted 18 months later. Unable to find a fall guy for the financial crisis, the American people and Congress set their sights on Goldman Sachs. The firm would have collapsed in September 2008 without a government rescue. Still, it paid employees $16.193 billion in 2009, or about $498,246 per employee, and rejected the idea that it ever "needed" a bailout. That same year, 4.74 million Americans lost their jobs.

So the public and its representatives turned their attention to Goldman Sachs, perhaps because the firm navigated the crisis more deftly than any of its peers. People often resent the rich more than they want vengeance on villains, and no one is richer in the public eye than Goldman Sachs, still benefiting in subtle ways from government support. During the crisis, it borrowed money with bonds guaranteed by the federal government, giving it a lower interest cost than otherwise would have been the case.

Eight decades ago the Senate Banking Committee's investigation into the causes of the Wall Street crash of 1929 resulted in the Glass-Steagall Act of 1933, separating commercial and investment banking, and the creation of the Securities and Exchange Commission. The work of the Pecora Commission, named for its chief counsel, Ferdinand Pecora, uncovered how the values on Wall Street in the 1920s seemed utterly incongruous to the public in the aftermath of The Crash of 1929. A similar pattern is playing out as this is being written (August 2010). Goldman's "competence" may come to be seen as a consequence of privileged access to market information and a willingness to use it without sharing this knowledge with its customer base. It may all be legal, but in public hearings it will be seen as bad form. Indeed, Goldman's traders made money every single month of the first quarter of 2010. Clients who followed the firm's recommended top trades for 2010 lost money in seven of the nine trades through May.

On April 16, 2010, the SEC filed suit against Goldman alleging it "defrauded investors by failing to disclose that a hedge-fund firm betting against them also played a role in creating what they bought." The suit alleged that Goldman created and sold the synthetic CDO linked to subprime mortgages without disclosing to investors that a hedge fund, Paulson & Co., helped pick the underlying securities and bet against the vehicle. Goldman denied any wrongdoing and settled the suit on July 16 within hours of President Obama signing the Dodd-Frank Act into law.

But Congress, the SEC, and the public still have their sights on Wall Street firms, and they are willing to dismantle them if necessary, even if they've done nothing wrong. Chris Dodd's bill creates a Financial Stability Oversight Council, which, among other things, could "Break Up Large, Complex Companies: Able to approve, with a two-thirds vote, a Federal Reserve decision to require a large, complex company, to divest itself of some of its holdings if it poses a grave threat to the financial stability of the United States but only as a last resort."

Something similar has happened before. In June 2002, Arthur Andersen, the auditor of Enron Corp., was convicted of obstruction of justice. The verdict effectively put the company out of business; the Supreme Court unanimously overturned the conviction three years later.

The Dodd-Frank Act may be law, but the regulators still have to write the rules. The Fed, the SEC, the CFTC, and others will craft the regulations over several years, which leaves plenty of time for lobbying and plenty of time to start devising ways to skirt the new rules.

What's Right with Wall Street?

Goldman may have become the public face of Wall Street during the financial crisis, but it doesn't resemble most other firms there, some of which are much smaller and privately held. Some have remained partnerships, and some start-ups are opting for structures that are reminiscent of the days when "customers' men" behaved like fiduciaries.

As the Goldman Sachs lawsuit makes clear, Wall Street needs an unconflicted business model. It is an untenable situation for firms to have inside knowledge of client intentions and orders then self-dealing to take advantage of that knowledge. The conflicts of interest need to be exposed. What's needed is an unconflicted model, a principles-based way of conducting business that is transparent for all stakeholders. Rules-based systems encourage participants to devise ways to skirt those rules. Doctors probably should not own hospitals, for example, and in no case should a taxpayer-supported doctor group be able to own a hospital. If a patient wants to go to doctors who own one, no government seal of approval should be there for the doctors' business. It's no secret that salespeople at auto dealerships are acting in their self-interest, not the buyers'. It should be equally clear that's the case in the financial markets. There are plenty of Wall Street firms that do make it clear. A few are profiled below.

Brown Brothers Harriman

In 1800 an Irish linen merchant named Alex Brown emigrated with his wife and sons to the United States from Ireland and settled in Baltimore, Maryland. He would later establish the first investment banking firm in the United States, which would arrange the first U.S. initial public offering, the Baltimore Water Company.[11] The firm also helped finance the first important railroad in the United States., the Baltimore & Ohio.[12] Brown's sons eventually started related businesses in various locations, including the forerunner of Brown Brothers Harriman & Co. in New York in 1818, which is still there today. When the partnership formed, commercial banks took deposits, made loans, did business in foreign exchange, and acted as investment bankers, underwriting and distributing corporate securities. When the passage of the 1933 banking act forced commercial and investment banking to separate, most of the private bankers gave up deposit banking in favor of investment banking. BBH did not.

Complete

And BBH did not make Bloomberg News's meticulously maintained list of banks receiving government bailout funds during the 2007–2009 financial crisis. Nor does it make the league list of underwriters of mortgage-backed securities. For two centuries, this firm has resisted the temptations that other, larger firms succumbed to: going public, packaging mortgages, making markets in credit derivatives, and investing in collateralized debt obligations backed by credit default swaps. And it steered clients from toxic investments at client seminars as well. The decisions stem from its business organization as well as its philosophy of being a "trusted adviser," serving clients globally in three main businesses: Investor Services, Investment & Wealth Management, and Banking & Advisory.

Organized as a partnership, the bank is one of the longest continuously operated companies in the United States and has approximately 4,000 professionals in 15 offices throughout North America, Europe, and Asia. Forty partners are spread across the globe, from New York to London to Dublin to Hong Kong to Tokyo to Luxemburg, and are personally responsible for the debts of the firm. Any partner can sign a deal that puts the others on the hook for any losses and as well as for a capital call in which the partners would have to contribute more capital to the firm. This sort of personal liability has a way of focusing the mind. In other words, there is no "other people's money" (as noted earlier in the book) with which to make business decisions. It's all each partner's capital and it's all on the line.

I am not advocating a return to some golden era of partnerships, nor am I suggesting that is the only way to restore some semblance of order to Wall Street. I am saying, however, that a principle that presupposes the partnership should be imposed on the Street: that of fiduciary duty.

Marketfield Asset Management

In what may be the most ill-timed mutual fund launch in history, Marketfield Asset Management opened for business the day after the Standard & Poor's 500 Index posted its all-time intraday high in October

2007. Michael Aronstein, Chief Investment Strategist, had a better-timed move earlier in his career when, after being fully invested in the stock market from January until August 1987, he and his partners reversed their position and bought 2,500 puts on the S&P 500 Index on the exact day the market topped, August 25, anticipating a market decline. Six weeks later the market crashed on Black Monday, October 19, 1987. The next day, Aronstein graced the front page of *USA Today*. "It was dumb luck," says Aronstein. Maybe. Marketfield has outperformed 99 percent of the mutual funds in its class since inception.

Aronstein could have organized Marketfield as a hedge fund and gotten paid 2 percent of assets and 20 percent of profits. Given his performance, he would have raked in millions in compensation. Hedge funds were a thriving business in 2007, with the number in the United States rising to a record 7,634, according to Chicago-based Hedge Fund Research Inc. He opted instead for a business model that made him a fiduciary for his clients. He became a Registered Investment Advisor under the Investment Advisor's Act of 1940 and serves as a fiduciary, which means he has to put clients' interests above his own.

Aronstein, 57, has been on Wall Street since 1979. A weekend blacksmith, he's scared more than a few people with the characteristic black-and-blue bruises on his hands after a weekend of heavy pounding to shape iron. One not scared off was Michael Shaoul, CEO of Oscar Gruss and Son, formed in 1918, nearly a century after Brown Brothers Harriman. Aronstein and Shaoul teamed up to form Marketfield Asset Management and opened to the public on October 11, 2007, within 24 hours of the intraday all-time high of the S&P 500 Index.

Aronstein is also an ardent proponent of injecting fiduciary duty into Wall Street and Washington. This doesn't mean he supports any new rules or regulations; far from it. Rather, he says the laws on the books are enough and simply need to be applied. For salespeople in Wall Street, he suggests they be subject to the Investment Advisors Act of 1940. It contains a principles-based system rather than rules of behavior. All that has to be done is to require securities "salespeople" or "wealth advisors" to register under the existing 1940 law, he says. If salespeople were designated as fiduciaries, they would have a clear incentive to be working on the client's behalf, not peddling the company's latest piece of Financial Origami. If salespeople were not even affiliated with the firm, it would be even easier to imagine this happening.

For corporate boards and officers of companies, he suggests personal liability. If they were liable for losses, they would make certain they understood the Financial Origami products their firms were peddling. Few things in life focus the mind like the possibility of losing everything. This won't prevent a Bernie Madoff Ponzi scheme from happening again, but the SEC didn't prevent it in the first place.

As for government officials, he says they should be fiduciaries of the public trust, forcing them to divulge any conflicts of interest and to be informed before passing laws and regulations. This would have prevented congressmen acting as cheerleaders for Fannie and Freddie in one year, and then having to bail them out the next.

Egan-Jones Co.

Sean Egan, president of Egan-Jones Ratings Co. in Haverford, Pennsylvania, says the financial crisis demonstrates the need for a "neutral, independent source for deriving prices for illiquid securities" that can be accepted by both sides of a transaction and free from the perception that they're driven by ulterior motives. In other words, an unconflicted model is needed for credit rating agencies, too. Presently, the largest have conflicts as discussed above. Egan-Jones has a different model.

The firm started in December 1992 as Red Flag Research, doing what its name suggests: alerting investors to red flags on the credit of companies. In December 1995 Egan teamed up with Bruce Jones, a 13-year veteran at Moody's, and began selling, or rather, offering to sell, ratings to institutional investors. Bruce Jones jokes that the only way he can remember the abbreviation NRSRO is "No Room, Standing Room Only," which is what the club of the ratings agencies were for a long time. It took the Worldcom catastrophe, which Egan-Jones rated non-investment grade on July 26, 2001, a full year before the firm filed for bankruptcy and a full 10 months before Moody's and S&P downgraded to non-investment grade. Gradually, the SEC began to "recognize" other, smaller rating agencies.

The firm charges investors, not issuers, for its ratings on corporate debt. Egan concedes that some of his firm's ratings "leak" out into the public domain, but attributes that to leakage and breakage any kind of company faces in the normal course of things. The firm has been approached by issuers offering to pay to have their securities rated; Egan-Jones declined. The firm has refused to accept payment by any issuers. This means Egan-Jones does not have access to the company's books the way other ratings agencies do. Rather, it has to rely solely on publicly available information. It has even rated some CDOs, and has done so with a negative rating. Here, too, it did not have access to the structures the way the other rating agencies did, yet it still managed to determine the securities were not investment grade. Egan says the Dodd-Frank bill simply offers window dressing to rating agencies and fails to get to the source of the problem: conflicts of interest. Egan says it would be ideal to have three or four firms like his, each offering to sell ratings to the buy side of the market.

These are just a few examples of firms that managed to avoid getting caught up in the Financial Origami products and the extreme of taking good ideas and running them into the ground. And these companies accomplished that with the laws and regulations on the books right now. New rules are coming, but Wall Street is sure to engage in more episodes of Financial Origami to skirt them. Investors should not be lulled into a sense of complacency.

Epilogue

Investment banking, proprietary trading, commission-driven sales, and Financial Origami all under one roof create a conflict of interest for Wall Street firms. The conflict arises from the competing interests of "taking care of the customer" versus "creating investment instruments with enough commission, bid-ask spread, and pricing opacity to make it worthwhile to produce and trade them with clients." The whole incentive structure on the Street has been the driving force behind almost every destructive product that hit the headlines during the financial crisis, from derivatives to supposedly low-volatility hedge fund strategies. The conflict explains the lobbying dollars spent by the Street to fight off any attempts to force its sales staff, wealth managers, financial advisers, private bankers, and others to be designated as fiduciaries, which demands the elimination of conflicted behaviors. The entire shift of all the private banks to product delivery models with higher immediate payoffs rather than simple fee-based asset management is coming back to haunt them.

The Dodd-Frank bill gave the SEC the power to make stockbrokers and other sales personnel become fiduciaries, but only after the agency conducts a six-month review of the matter. Regardless of whether the SEC recommends such a move, investors will come to realize that they have alternatives to the traditional brokerage houses, the biggest of which now reside in commercial banks. The main alternatives are fee-only advisory shops, most of which have avoided nearly all of the toxic investments because they have no incentives at all to seek complexity. The exodus to these registered investment advisers is already happening. Banks managed $4.2 trillion for their clients at the end of 2009 (the latest data available), down from $5.5 trillion a year earlier, according to figures from Cerulli Associates. That's a 24 percent decline in a year that the S&P 500 *gained* 23 percent! In the first half of 2010 alone, Charles Schwab Advisor Services reported $8 billion in net new assets from newly independent advisors, up 60 percent compared to the same period in 2009. The figure represents more than one-third of the total $25 billion in such assets that flowed into Schwab Advisor Services in the first two quarters of 2010. Some 42 percent of newly independent advisers in 2010 have chosen to join existing RIA firms versus starting their own.

Goldman Sachs may be the poster child for public anger at Wall Street investment banks. And Citigroup may epitomize a lot of how and why the Wall Street Model broke. The merger of Citicorp, founded as City Bank of New York in 1812, and insurance giant Travelers Group Inc. (which included bond trader Salomon Brothers and broker Smith Barney) in 1998 forced the hand of regulators, who approved the deal. This set the stage for the formal repeal of the Glass-Steagall Act the following year. Citigroup, the combined company's new name, was the largest U.S. bank by assets at the onset of the financial crisis; it was also extraordinarily leveraged. At the end of 2002, when Citi paid $400 million in the global analyst settlement, when the bull market in stocks began, and when Wall Street firms began to manufacture risk, Citigroup held $1.1 trillion in assets: 12.7 times its $86.7 billion in equity. By the end of 2007 it held $2.2 trillion, or 19.7 times its $114 billion in equity. Assets rose by 100 percent while equity supporting it rose only 31 percent. It was also the

Epilogue

biggest U.S. financial services company: the biggest credit card company, the second-biggest wealth manager, and the biggest corporate securities underwriter all under one roof.

We saw earlier that Citi was at the heart of the conflict of interest problems with analysts during the dot-com boom, paying the bulk of the global settlement of analysts touting stocks they privately thought were bad investments all in order to get investment banking business. Those were some of the first cracks in the foundation of Wall Street's business model, cracks that grew over the next five years despite a bull market in stocks.

On Sunday, October 15, 2007, five years after the start of the bull market, Citigroup, JP Morgan, and Bank of America announced the creation of an $80 billion fund to enhance liquidity in the market for asset-backed commercial paper and medium-term notes issued by SIVs they had sponsored. The new fund would buy assets from the sponsored SIVs, which were finding it increasingly difficult to fund themselves. That ran the risk that they would dump their $320 billion of investments, driving down prices. On October 12, the S&P 500 index had posted its record intraday high and a new bear market had begun, even if market participants did not recognize at the time. The liquidity fund was just one more act of Financial Origami: effectively creating a new "Super SIV" to purchase the assets of other SIVs that were having difficulty rolling over their debt. The banks decided against the Super-SIV on December 21, 2007, and instead began to buy back the impaired assets in the SIVs, taking write downs and losses in the process.

The bear market in stocks and the spreading of the subprime crisis into something larger were both well under way when Lehman collapsed September 15, 2008. Investor panic intensified when the Reserve Primary Fund shares broke the buck the next day on Lehman's bankruptcy, and it would persist until Citigroup shares broke the buck March 5, 2009. Within 24 hours, the S&P 500 Index bottomed on an intraday basis and the and subsequent bull market emerged even if people didn't recognize it at the time. In all, the 17-month bear market in global stocks erased $40 trillion in wealth.

On the day the S&P made its bear market intra day low, March 6, former Federal Reserve Chairman Paul Volcker, of the "Saturday Night Massacre" fame, said commercial banks should be separated from investment banks in order to avoid another crisis. "Maybe we ought to have a kind of two-tier financial system," Volcker, who at the time headed President Barack Obama's Economic Recovery Advisory Board, said at a conference at New York University's Stern School of Business. In Volcker's view, commercial banks would be highly regulated and allowed to provide customers with depositary services and access to credit. Securities firms would have the freedom to take on more risk and trading and be "relatively free of regulation." It sounds like a throwback to the Glass-Steagall era. That may not be a bad thing. It's even possible that some banks will come to that conclusion on their own and migrate to that model with or without new rules and regulations.

I am not arguing either for more or less regulation. Some of the most heavily regulated firms were at the center of the financial crisis, and some of the least at the periphery, so more regulation doesn't necessarily guarantee success. And regulations also trigger more Financial Origami to circumvent the rules imposed. Politicians cannot legislate or regulate moral character into existence. Still, as we saw, there are already companies managing to do it as fiduciaries and with unconflicted models so no new are rules needed.

There is a lot to learn from the firms that avoided the business models that wreaked so much havoc on the financial system. Brown Brothers Harriman is a "trusted adviser" to its clients and does not engage in proprietary trading. Marketfield manages other people's money under a fiduciary standard, with its broad principles-based approach rather than a rules-based one. Egan-Jones has an unconflicted model of selling of ratings to investors instead of issuers. The fact that these firms and others like them avoided the products and strategies others succumbed to suggests there are enough rules on the books as is. Doubtless, regulators will write hundreds more rules to comply with the Dodd-Frank Act. As regulators go about writing the rules, they should be aware of what's been said in this book—namely, that regulation spawns Financial Origami as actors work to skirt the new rules. A principles-based environment is more effective. And investors would do well to recall Christopher Dodd's acknowledgment that no legislation can stop the next crisis from coming. If salespeople were designated as fiduciaries under existing laws, they would have a clear incentive to be working on the client's behalf, and not to peddle the company's latest piece of Financial Origami. If companies didn't have a captive sales force willing to cram new products through that system, less and perhaps none of it would happen. If salespeople were not affiliated with the firm, it would be even easier to imagine this happening.

Given the prevalence of Financial Origami on Wall Street, I would add that for every investment product bought, investors should get answers as to what part equity, what part debt, and what part insurance the product price represents. If investors were told that the "price" of a synthetic CDO (a securitized liability) might be as high as their entire investment, whether AAA-rated or not, at least that will have been divulged and the investors can better decide whether to invest.

Notes

Introduction

1. Eichengreen, Barry. *Globalizing Capital*. Princeton: Princeton University Press, 1996, p. 3.

Chapter 1: Fold Sides to Center

1. In 1994 an institutional money market mutual fund, Community Bankers U.S. Government Fund, broke the buck.
2. Taleb, Nassim Nicholas. *The Black Swan*. New York: Random House, 2007.
3. Bureau of Economic Analysis.
4. Bagehot, Walter. *Lombard Street*. Springfield, MA: Seven Treasures Publications, 2009, p. 108. Originally published 1873.
5. Popper, Margaret, and Onaran, Yalman. "Bank of America Said to Walk Away from Lehman Talks." *Bloomberg News* (September 14, 2008).

Chapter 2: Result, Turn Over

1. Markowitz, Harry. "Portfolio Selection." *The Journal of Finance,* Vol. 7, No. 1 (March 1952), pp. 77–91.
2. Aristotle. *Politics*. Harmondsworth, United Kingdowm: Penguin, 1957, p. 90.

153

3. Scholes, Myron. "Derivatives in a Dynamic Environment." Nobel Prize acceptance speech. December 1997. Available at http://nobelprize.org/nobel_prizes/economics/laureates/1997/scholes-lecture.pdf, accessed April 5, 2010.

Chapter 3: Fold Sides to Center, Again

1. Miller, Merton. "Financial Innovation: The Last Twenty Years and the Next." *Journal of Quantitative and Financial Analysis,* Vol. 21, No. 4 (December 1986).
2. Ibid.

Chapter 4: Fold Tip to Point

1. Harper, Christine. "Wall Street Shareholders Suffer Losses Partners Never Imagined." *Bloomberg News* (February 10, 2008).
2. Ibid.
3. Ibid.
4. Ibid.
5. Ibid.
6. Ibid.
7. Dunbar, Nicholas. *Inventing Money.* New York: Wiley, 2001, p. 65.

Chapter 5: Fold Point Back

1. Wells, Rob, and Rega, John. "Congress Approves Bill Letting Banks, Brokers, Insurers Merge." *Bloomberg News* (November 9, 1999).
2. Tweed, David. "Value of Global Stocks Surpasses Value of World Output." *Bloomberg News* (December 23, 1999).
3. Blankfein, Lloyd. "Do Not Destroy the Essential Catalyst of Risk." *Financial Times* (February 9, 2009).

Chapter 6: Fold in Half

1. Wells, David. "The Revenge of the Bond Traders." *Bloomberg Markets* (March 2003), p. 26.
2. Morgenson, Gretchen, and Story, Louise. "Rating Agency Data Aided Wall Street in Deals." *New York Times* (April 24, 2010).

Chapter 7: Pull Neck Upright

1. Wells, David. "Bond Traders with Math, Physics Degrees Rise in Pecking Order." *Bloomberg News* (January 30, 2003).

Notes

2. Ibid.

3. Greenspan, Alan. "World Finance and Risk Management." At Lancaster House, London, U.K. September 25, 2002. Speech available at http://www.federalreserve.gov/boarddocs/speeches/2002/200209253/default.htm.

4. James Stock, a Harvard economist, coined the phrase "the great moderation" while writing a research paper with Mark Watson of Princeton. "Has the Business Cycle Changed and Why." Available at http://ideas.repec.org/p/nbr/nberwo/9127.html, accessed November 22, 2010.

5. Drucker, Peter. *Management.* New York: Harper Row, 1985, p. 512.

6. Courdert, Virgine, and Gex, Mathieu. "Stormy Weather in the Credit Default Swap Market." p. 203. Available at http://www.voxeu.org/reports/reinhart_felton_vol2/First_Global_Crisis_Vol2.pdf, accessed November 22, 2010.

7. Braudel, Fernand. *The Wheels of Commerce.* Los Angeles: University of California Press, 1992, pp. 44, 47.

8. Leising, Matthew. "CME Group's Futures Traders Object to Bailing Out Default Swaps." *Bloomberg News* (February 11, 2010).

Chapter 8: Pull Head to Suitable Angle

1. For a full treatment of these activities, see *What I Learned Losing A Million Dollars,* by Jim Paul and Brendan Moynihan. Nashville: Infrared Press, 1994, pp. 85–100.

2. Greenspan, Alan. "The Crisis " March 9, 2010, p. 7. Available at http://www.brookings.edu/~/media/files/programs/es/bpea/2010_spring_bpea_papers/spring2010_greenspan.pdf, accessed November 22, 2010.

3. Ibid, p. 7.

4. Desroches, Brigitte, and Francis, Michael. "World Real Interest Rates: A Global Savings and Investment Perspective." Bank of Canada Working Paper (March 2007).

5. Bjerga, Alan, and Leising, Matt. "Cotton-Price Swings Prompt Probe by U.S. Regulator" *Bloomberg News* (June 3, 2008).

6. *BIS Quarterly Review,* September 2008, pp. 69–70.

Chapter 9: Complete

1. Dodd, Christopher. Press conference, March 15, 2010. Transcript. Copyright 2010 Roll Call, Inc.

2. Ibid.

3. Davis, Ann. "Trader Hits Jackpot in Oil, as Commodity Boom Roars On." *The Wall Street Journal* (February 28, 2008).

4. President George W. Bush address to the White House Conference on Increasing Minority Homeownership at The George Washington University, October 15, 2002.

5. Greenspan, Alan. "The Crisis." March 9, 2010, p. 7. Available at http://www.brookings.edu/~/media/files/programs/es/bpea/2010_spring_bpea_papers/spring2010_greenspan.pdf, accessed November 22, 2010.

6. Woellert, Lorraine, and Gittelsohn, John. "Fannie–Freddie Fix at $160 Billion with $1 Trillion Worst Case." *Bloomberg News* (June 10, 2010).

7. Smith, Elliot Blair. " 'Race to Bottom' at Moody's, S&P Secured Subprime's Boom, Bust." *Bloomberg News* (September 14, 2008).

8. Smith, Elliot Blair. "Bringing Down Wall Street as Ratings Let Loose Subprime Scourge." *Bloomberg News* (September 23, 2008).

9. Woellert and Gittelson, op. cit.

10. Harper, Christine. "Taxpayers Help Goldman Reach Height of Profit in New Skyscraper." *Bloomberg News* (December 20, 2009).

11. Early History of Deutschebank Alex Brown http://www.pwm.db.com/pwm/en/contact-us-alex_brown.html, accessed November 22, 2010.

12. Kouwenhoven, John A. *Partners in Banking.* Garden City, NY: Doubleday & Company, 1968, p. 71.

About the Author

Brendan Moynihan is an editor-at-large for Bloomberg News, where he manages the popular Chart of the Day column and writes about the economy and Wall Street. A 20-year veteran of Wall Street as a trader, he also taught finance at Vanderbilt University. He is the author of *Trading on Expectations* (Wiley, 1997) and co-author of *What I Learned Losing A Million Dollars* (Infrared Press, 1994). He lives in Barrington Hills, Illinois, with his wife and two sons, and is writing a book on English grammar.

Index

Index

Index

Index

Index

Index

W

Wall Street
  agent-driven/principal-driven
    departments, competition,
    93–94
  competitiveness, increase, 54
  copulas formula, usage, 81
  firms, public appearance, 51f
  horizontal industry, 48f
  insurance, risk-sharing business,
    43–44
  one-stop shopping, vertically
    integrated industry, 49f
  paper, folding, 27f
  potential, 141–146
  primary market, 12f
  problems, 130
  profits, increase, 106
  regulatory environment change
    (1971/1981), 37–38
  risk-transfer business/products, 13, 19

  risk transfer instruments, 38f
  rules/refold/rave/ruin pattern,
    64–66
  secondary market, 13f
  structured products, creation,
    137–138
Washington Mutual, bankruptcy, 15
White shoe partnerships, 47–48
Wilshire 5000 Index, peak
    (2000), 53
World Bank, dollar-denominated
    interest payments, 37
WorldCom, Inc.
  accounting fraud scandal,
    129–130
  bankruptcy, 95

Y

Y2K millennium computer bug,
    preparation, 67
Yield reach, 69